Edward de Bono studied at Christ Church, Oxford (as a Rhodes Scholar). He also holds a PhD from Cambridge and an MD from the University of Malta. He has held appointments at the universities of Oxford, London, Cambridge and Harvard.

In 1967 de Bono invented the now commonly used term 'lateral thinking' and, for many thousands, indeed millions, of people worldwide, his name has since become a symbol of creativity and new thinking. He has written numerous books, which have been translated into 34 languages, and his advice is sought by Nobel laureates and world leaders alike.

FUTURE
POSITIVE

Edward de Bono

Vermilion
LONDON

3 5 7 9 10 8 6 4 2

Vermilion, an imprint of Ebury Publishing,
20 Vauxhall Bridge Road,
London SW1V 2SA

Vermilion is part of the Penguin Random House group of companies whose
addresses can be found at global.penguinrandomhouse.com

Penguin
Random House
UK

This edition first published in the United Kingdom by Vermilion in 2017
First published by Maurice Temple Smith Ltd 1979

www.penguin.co.uk

A CIP catalogue record for this book is available from the British Library

ISBN 9781785041099

Printed and bound in Great Britain by Clays Ltd, St Ives PLC

Penguin Random House is committed to a sustainable future for our business,
our readers and our planet. This book is made from Forest Stewardship
Council® certified paper.

MIX
Paper from
responsible sources
FSC® C018179

CONTENTS

FOREWORD

This book was written in eight days in the summer of 1978 while I was staying with Vera and Philip Le Cras at their delightful house in Jersey and I am most grateful to them for providing the atmosphere that made it possible to write the book in such a short time.

I mention this short time not as a boast nor as an excuse although I appreciate it may very reasonably be construed as both. I mention it more as an explanation and as an instruction to the reader to read through the book in the same manner as it was written. Go through the book lightly stepping on each concept before moving on to the next one. Do not expect each idea to carry the full weight of solemn pounding. There may be times when you do wish to pause and to examine in detail the implications of a particular concept. In that case you must use your own thinking and do much more than just react to what I have set down. You may see positive possibilities which have escaped me. That you may see dangerous implications which I have not set down is very probable. But do not let those pitfalls bring your exploration to an end.

It is said that one ought to visit a country for three days or for thirty years. In three days you get a general impression and it may take thirty years to get a true picture. In between you will get distortion as you pursue each aspect in detail. If I had to spend thirty years writing this book it would still be too short a time to do justice to the subject but the book would not be much better for it would be so weighted down with qualifications and hesitations that the brashness of provocation would be quite lost.

1 INTRODUCTION

There is much to be said for being realistically gloomy about the future and not much to be said for being irresponsibly cheerful. If you are gloomy you are unlikely to be proved wrong by history and you can also feel that you have done a useful service by shocking society into mending its ways in order to avoid the looming disaster. Yet I believe the future will be positive and even marvellous.

It is only fair to say that this positive view of the future is not supported by present trends. A huge increase in crime threatens the fabric of society. Every month one thousand Londoners are wounded in personal attacks with knives or coshes or firearms. Every day 478 cars are stolen in London. Last year there was a 23 per cent increase in violent crime. In Italy ex-premier Aldo Moro was kidnapped and murdered by the Red Brigade. Twenty-two German dentists drive in their Mercedes cars to a Dentists' Conference in Milan – eighteen of their cars are stolen. On a world scale we continue to use up energy and material resources at a fast rate with only a slight reduction in the rate of oil consumption following the rise in its price. We are almost as careless about pollution as ever. Adding copper to a pig's feed increases the profit per bacon pig by £2.72 so farmers resist the recommendation to reduce the amount of copper added to reduce the risk of polluting the soil where the pig slurry is disposed of. The world population will climb to

6.3 billion (from 4 billion today) by the end of the century and to 8 billion by 2020. The World Bank estimates that there are 600 million people living today in absolute poverty. Even in progressive Brazil there are said to be 30 million people with annual incomes of only $77. We seem set to use nuclear fuel and its contamination hazards. Nuclear confrontation remains a permanent threat.

It seems that bit by logical bit we have built up a Frankenstein monster which has acquired a system-life of its own and is beyond our control. As with the weather we can observe it and chart its progress but remain unable to alter it. We can take temporary shelter from the storms and crises but we seem powerless to prevent them.

Does there come a point at which power and complexity take over and the world system hastens, out of control, to inevitable disaster? Certainly we have the complexity. There was a time when government leaders were able to understand the world they were supposed to govern. Then, as matters got more complex, the leaders had to call on expert advisers but were still able to comprehend the options open to them. Today, matters are too complex even for that. How many government leaders really understand the implications of nuclear power when even the experts are undecided as to how to treat the peculiar types of risk involved? And when the experts are in disagreement – as they so often are in economic matters – how are politicians to choose their strategy? The best they can do is to stand close to their supporters and to protect their supporters from obvious harm. That is a different matter from leadership. How many people can foresee the later consequences of an economic choice? What would be the effect on investment of lowering a high tax-rate? There are so many variables, interactions and feedback loops that educated guesswork is the best forecast. In 1918 there were 180 pages of tax acts in the UK and today there are over 4,000 pages. That figure parallels the increasing complexity in all fields of society. A business employing about 3,000 people has to fill in more than 357 government forms each year.

The population of India increases each year by an amount equal to the total population of Australia. About four times the population of Switzerland passes through Heathrow airport each year.

It seems that any step in apparently the right direction only increases the complexity of the problems. An improvement in health care leads to a fall in infant and adult mortality and a population explosion. The development of nuclear energy increases the hazards of pollution.

The speed of change increases all the time but the human life span does not. From the first aeroplane to the Concorde that travels at twice the speed of a rifle bullet, took less than one lifetime. From the first primitive atomic bomb to super-bombs only half a lifetime. From the first space journey to landing on the moon only a quarter of a lifetime.

Our productive capacity is enormous. In the twenty-five years to 1973 world industrial output quadrupled. One man in agriculture can now produce as much as it took one thousand men to do a couple of centuries ago. With so much positive achievement have we indeed created an uncontrollable Frankenstein system?

It would be easy to write a book that laid the blame for world problems on blind scientists or greedy politicians or industrialised countries indifferent to the plight of the Third World. It would be easy to claim that if everyone mended their ways the future would really be positive. But in the approach I am going to take there are no villains. There are only highly intelligent people acting from moment to moment with the greatest good sense. In practice this may not strictly be true but I wish to suggest that our problems are not due to stupidity, but to the exercise of intelligence.

Some weeks ago I invented a rather simple puzzle which involved putting together sixteen small squares to form one large square. Each small square had a design on both of its faces. Simple as the problem is, it can take rather a long time to solve. If you made one 'move' every second playing day and night, it could take you one thousand million years to solve the problem. The reason is that you cannot tell you have solved the problem until the last piece has been put into position – and the number of possible trial and error variations is mathematically enormous. It would be easy to solve the problem if at each moment we had some way of telling which was the right move to make – as we have in a jigsaw puzzle. In that case the problem would be solved in seconds. But we do not have such an indication and a piece which appears to be the right one at the moment can make things quite impossible later.

Unfortunately the world problems are more similar to my squares puzzle than to an ordinary jigsaw. We do not really know the right move to make at any moment. So in the course of the development of our civilisation we have evolved a simple – and effective – strategy. We have created certain basic principles and at each decision point we choose the course of action that satisfies these principles. We feel that in this way we cannot go wrong and that the accumulation of decisions will lead us further towards the goal of civilisation. The basic principles that we always seek to follow are the basic principles of civilisation such as: respect for human life; justice; freedom and the other matters encoded in the constitution of the United States of America. To these basic principles might be added other principles of a more political nature like the principle of equality or the distribution of wealth. These are all positive principles so far. But the system works just as well for negative principles such as a dislike of capitalism or a dislike of authoritarianism. We do not regard the total assembly of principles as a magical utopia which we shall one day reach. We regard them as principles to be applied at every decision point so that we shall find ourselves heading in the right direction.

Imagine an exploration party in a land-rover making its way across the Sahara desert. It is not possible to set a course in a straight line and then stick to this because some of the sand dunes are too high to climb and must be detoured around. But the navigator has his compass and at each decision point he tells the driver to head North. They know that if they keep heading North they cannot go wrong. So this general 'direction' of North corresponds to the basic principles that we use at our decision points as we navigate towards a greater degree of civilisation. In the absence of a map the strategy would appear to be simple, effective and foolproof. But, alas, it is not.

Unfortunately the world we live in is not like a trackless desert but more like a pattern of roads in the countryside. We cannot travel freely in any direction but must stick to the roads. The roads correspond to the structures and institutions we have developed in our society. There are political structures and commercial structures and when we act we have to follow the direction of action of the various structures that exist. We have parliamentary structures and financial structures and legal structures and media structures. These structures are social institutions which exist as organisations in the world around us. But we also have structures in our minds. These mental structures result from the way we organise the world around us into concepts. These structure concepts are usually well established in our society and include concepts like profit, capital, justice and democracy.

So in the analogy we transfer the land-rover from the desert to the countryside and we suppose that it is still heading for a destination that lies North. Does the strategy still hold? Is it enough for the navigator to tell the driver to take the North-pointing road at each junction – and to avoid taking roads that head South? It is not. Let us take the most extreme case, which is a motorway running from East to West and curving slightly Northwards. Our land-rover party is driving, in the United

Kingdom, from the East. The driver notices that there is a road leading off the motorway and pointing due South. For some reason the sign is unreadable. He knows that the basic strategy does not allow him to take South-pointing roads so he proceeds along the motorway and never finds a turning that points North. Of course all junctions that eventually lead North are South-pointing where they leave the motorway. This is an extreme example but the point is simple: in a road system it may often be necessary to temporarily travel South in order to eventually find your way North. But a strategy that insists you move Northward at every instance does not allow this.

It is easy to see why civilisation cannot allow the temporary movement to the South or a temporary movement against its basic principles. Such an acceptance would signify that the end justified the means – that it was permitted to move against the basic principles if the ultimate objective was to move in the direction of the principles (that is to say moving South in order to eventually move North). Terrorists always justify their killing of innocent civilians on the basis that the end – the political objective – justifies the means. Dictators imprison their political opponents on the same basis for the objective of political stability justifies the imprisonment. The bombing of Dresden, Hiroshima and Nagasaki may, philosophically, be no different. But the acceptance of the principle that the end justifies the means is too dangerous since it destroys the basic principles themselves. Any person who wishes to go against the principles has only to pretend an ultimate goal that follows the principles.

For a long time Sweden has been a caring socialist state and Switzerland a capitalist one. Although the populations and history are not widely different, today Sweden has 97,000 unemployed and Switzerland has 7,627. There is relatively little social welfare in Japan so the Japanese save heavily for illness or a rainy day. These savings have fuelled industrial development with the result that today the Japanese workers are apparently better off than their counterparts in the United Kingdom. These are incomplete examples because the measure of 'being better off' is debatable. But they do illustrate that sometimes in order to go 'North' you may have to journey 'South' for a while. But the principle – real though it is – cannot be applied. Unless you had a sound map you could never convince yourself that going South was the best strategy at that point for moving Northwards. So the dilemma is set.

Evolution moves forwards not backwards. Mistakes can be made but it is not possible to take a negative step that moves consciously against the direction of improvement. Evolution in society is towards the perfection and interlocking of its institutions and concepts. Once set up these have a momentum of their own and in the interplay of their actions they become meshed into an integral stable whole.

The dinosaur was a remarkably successful creature. Man has only been around for some ten million years but the dinosaur survived for a hundred and thirty million years. So when we regard the dinosaur as a classic failure of adaptation we are looking at the moment of failure rather than at the many years of success. Right up until the moment of failure the dinosaur was a success. But hindsight satisfaction with success was no protection against extinction in the future. Furthermore, right up to the end the various parts of the dinosaur were carrying out their evolved function in perfect order: the heart, the brain, the muscles and sinews were all performing as competently as ever. So neither a successful history nor physiological soundness was sufficient to guarantee the dinosaur a future in its evolved state. The one evolutionary quality it had not got was that of adaptation. But it was its very success over a hundred and thirty million years that had perfected its structure.

So we see that neither conscious decision nor evolutionary momentum can allow society to move away from the direction that became set in the past under perhaps rather different circumstances. It is not a failure of intelligence or good sense. Neither is it a weakness or malfunction in the institutions that, like the dinosaur's bones and muscles, go to make up the whole.

We are not sure of the precise change of circumstance that brought the successful dinosaur to its end. There may have been one major change or one minor but vital change or a series of small changes each of which was unimportant in itself but which, taken together, killed off the dinosaur. Quite possibly the dinosaur was conscious of the changes but unable to do anything about them for it was locked into its perfected evolutionary state.

We do, however, know the changed circumstances that face society today. They are changes in power, speed and magnitude. We have to cope more quickly than ever and with problems that are much bigger and with an order of complexity much greater than ever before. At the same time mistakes can be fatal: for example in nuclear power or genetic engineering or gradual pollution. We have less time in which to make decisions and less time in which to muddle through change by trial and error.

Basically the problem is one of complexity. Changes in the technology of communication increase complexity by allowing the development of feedback loops. Changes in power increase complexity by extending the ripples of effect that spread through society.

By great good fortune, and just in time, we have to hand a device that can rescue us from the mess of complexity. That device is the computer. The computer will be to the organisation revolution what steam power was to the industrial revolution. The computer can extend our organising power in the same way as steam extended muscle power.

The benefits of the computer will not be seen if we simply use them – as we are doing – to save us from the inefficiency of our current way of doing things. The advantage of the computer is that it allows us to develop totally different systems of organisation. Just as the motor car allowed the development of motor car based cities like Los Angeles, so the computer allows the development of computer based organisation. Of course we have to ensure that the result is more human rather than less human. Similarly we have to use the computer to reduce complexity rather than to increase complexity, by making it possible to cope with increased complexity. An example of a computer based organisation is air travel which, given the huge volumes involved, is remarkably safe and efficient. Both the design of aeroplanes, and the running of them, have depended on the computer. Air traffic control, scheduling, the logistics of reservations, all depend on computer handling.

We cannot depend on the computer experts to provide the ideas, for in my experience they are – with exceptions – remarkably unimaginative. This is no fault of their own for in a rapidly expanding field a spurious orthodoxy quickly develops: 'define the problem, find the standard solution, apply it'. In essence a computer expert left to himself would design an ingenious computerised leg rather than the wheel.

Can we then expect that a combination of good-will, intelligence, problem-solving skill and the computer will solve the problems facing man today? To my mind the answer is almost certainly negative. We have not lacked good-will or intelligence or problem-solving ability. And all the computer will do is to provide for the more efficient exercise of these.

The trouble is that, like the car on the road and the dinosaur with its anatomy, we are locked into structures that determine our freedom of action. In practice these structures are the institutions we have and – even more importantly – the concepts and habits of thinking that structure our mind. We must note that the airline system developed so effectively because it did not have to battle with established structures and concepts.

Of one thing we can be sure. The quality of our life in the future will be determined by the quality of our thinking.

2 MECHANISMS OF CHANGE

None of the mechanisms of change outlined below are exclusive. There is a good deal of overlap and sometimes one mode of change may alter into another. Change itself is only a virtue if it leads to something better or if it is demanded by an alteration in circumstances. Societies change because there are internal forces that lead to change or in order to cope with an altered world or in order to improve the lot of their citizens. Change may be in the direction of a doctrinal utopia or simply to restore a status quo that has been eroded by circumstance.

Change by salvation and desperation

The basic principle is to do nothing and to hope that before things really get bad a new technological development will offer salvation. For example we hope that a development in nuclear fusion technology will rescue us from a final depletion of oil resources – or a new way of using coal more conveniently. Similarly we hope that a change in birth control technology will make it possible to limit population growth in the Third World. Desperation works in the same way. When the crisis really hits then something will have to be done about it: effort will be focused and the public will be behind the effort. The strategy has several advantages especially in terms of reducing the need to do anything at the moment. But some problems are irreversible. For example a crisis level of pollution may be irreversible for though future pollution may be stopped, the existing level may be unalterable.

Change by crisis management and drift

This is the method favoured in most political systems. Whenever a crisis occurs it is blamed on the external world and the government of the day is seen to be making valiant efforts to solve it. That the crisis may actually have arisen from previous policies is not mentioned. Problem solving skills are focused and a solution of sorts is found. Political expediency triumphs for the moment. In between the episodes of crisis management there is a general drift determined by the shifting power-groups in society and changes in attitudes and values. Politicians see themselves not as navigating the boat of society but as surviving the storms that arise from time to time. It is enough that a politician should be seen to have his heart in the right place and a bailing-pump in good order. Each crisis that is coped with does not completely restore the status quo. There is a residue. Legislation introduced to solve the problem tends to stay on the statute books. So to the underlying drift there is added the change produced by crisis residue. This is not to suggest that such crises are deliberately used as opportunities to introduce deliberate changes – though this can happen as well.

Change by evolution

This can be nothing more than a polite description of the change method described before: one man's drift is another man's evolution. True evolution is essentially a shift of emphasis. One thing atrophies whilst another hypertrophies. There are shifts of power, shifts of activity and shifts of values. These are thwarted or encouraged by the structure of the society and the nature of its institutions. In economic terms a market economy is supposed to allow true change by evolution – and all else to hinder this.

Change by protest

Change by protest supposes that those running the system are endowed with intelligence, vigour and resources. The purpose of the protest is to modify the behaviour of those in control: to restrict it in certain areas and to direct it into other areas. In such matters as ecology protest has been remarkably successful. The power of the media, and especially of television, serves to amplify a small protest into a major one. A protest that may initially be very small has to be bizarre enough to guarantee media attention. Once there is exposure then others jump on the bandwagon and the movement grows. Politicians who are looking for areas of exposure join the bandwagon if it is positive and react to it if it is negative. So the system works in a most effective way. In the United Kingdom a man was released from prison because a small group of friends protested his innocence loudly enough. The only disadvantage of the system is that the importance of the matter – or even the validity of the issue – has little to do with the effectiveness of the protest. Unpopular but important issues cannot use the system. Any emotional issue can. By and large, protest tends to be negative although its ultimate results are positive. For example protest against pollution is in favour of ecology and Ralph Nader's famous protest against unsafe cars is in favour of safer cars. If the protest is a good political bandwagon then the reaction may be excessive; for example in California the environment protection requirements are so strict as to hold up business development and employment prospects. In some circumstances a noisy minority can impose their wishes on a quiet majority.

Change by resistance and ultimate retreat

The threatened change is resisted as long as possible. There is no attempt to anticipate change and then to move with it. This delay and resistance allows the direction of change to become very clear. It also allows others to make the change and provide an experiment that can be observed. In the industrial world there is often a deliberate 'me-too' policy: let someone else bear the costs of development and make the initial mistakes – then make the change yourself. Finally when the pent-up change is inevitable you withdraw resistance and move swiftly with it. The retreat of Great Britain from its Empire was a classic example of this sort of change.

Change by alternatives

This is supposed to be the method that works in any democracy. The opposition party puts forward an alternative policy to the governing party and if the electorate prefer the alternative they vote in the opposition at the next electoral opportunity. But, for a variety of reasons, it does not quite work that way. Any party in opposition knows that to get back into power it must not only hold its own supporters but also capture some of the floating voters or other party voters. So the alternatives get less and less different and in the end no true alternative is offered. Furthermore in a complex world the same experts make the economic analyses and so the proposed policies end up by being quite similar. In most democratic countries today it is quite hard to see the real differences in the policies offered by the opposing parties. The similarity will probably get greater as it becomes less possible to undo policies set in motion by previous governments. It is only in countries like the UK where the parties have an historical class base that differences of policy can exist.

Change by compromise

A camel is said to be a horse designed by a committee. So change by compromise is change by bargaining in which each interested party seeks to have its own proposal represented in the final outcome. It is pork-barrel politics in the traditional style of the US Congress. It is also the style of change in countries that elect their representatives by proportional representation with the result that government is by coalition. By far the majority of labour disputes in industry are solved on the basis of compromise. So what precedes the compromise may be a dispute or the input of a minor party seeking to exert its identity.

Change by Hegelian clash

First there is a thesis. Then an anti-thesis forms in opposition to the thesis. From the dynamic tensions created by the clash emerges the synthesis which is a changed order of things. In theory this works, but in practice it does not. It would work if both sides were seeking the best features from the other point of view in order to build up a synthesis that would be better than either alone. In practice the antithesis team derive most of their energy and direction by simply being against everything on the 'thesis' side – with the result that destruction of every aspect of the existing order becomes the objective.

Change by revolution

The old order is destroyed and a new one sweeps in to take its place. Revolution in France, revolution in Russia, revolution in Cuba. My system is better than yours and in any case yours is worse than mine. Your system is full of corruption and exploitation and privilege. My system is for the good of the people. The revolution is to be achieved by direct struggle of one sort or another. Creeping revolution is not good enough because the sharpness of the change will be lost even though each of the aims may be perfectly achieved. Sometimes it is enough to sabotage the old system so that it will collapse into chaos, and phoenix-like from this chaos will arise the new order. For many revolution is a direction and not a destination. Many a revolutionary would rather follow his revolutionary fervour in a country he wished to change than go to live in a country where the change had already been achieved. The difference may be that between an entrepreneur and a manager. Protest as a means towards revolution needs to be carefully distinguished from protest as a means towards improving the behaviour of the existing system. The latter is really a vote of confidence in the system.

Change by leadership

A de Gaulle arises to change France and to change Europe. Change by leadership is change by decision and change by inspiration. The leader is in the same position as a chief executive in a corporation. With an eye to the future and to the capabilities of his corporation he makes decisions by decree. How much he listens to his advisers, how much his decisions are fed by personal vanity, how much he is corrupted by power are all quite separate from the functional exercise of the power of change. Because the system is so effective it suffers all the dangers that go with unrestrained effectiveness. After all the chief executive is somewhat restrained by the views of the other executives, his stockholders and the financial press. He can also be dismissed. It may be that the power to inspire is enough in a leader even when it is not accompanied by executive control. Mahatma Gandhi in India might have been an example of such leadership. But leadership in protest is not quite the same as leadership in operation and administration. Protest is its own achievement.

Change by inspiration

Inspiration by a charismatic leader, by a new religion, by an old religion revived, by a new idea and by desperate circumstances are obvious mechanisms of change. Over the last one hundred years the attitude in both the USA and Europe towards Africans has undergone a total revolution. In many quarters the attitude towards business has also undergone a revolution. The process is extremely powerful but difficult to control and to predict.

Change by degrees

It is difficult to tell whether changes in attitude are brought about by inspired leaders or by an accumulation of tiny steps: change by degrees. Just as the stock-market rises because each little step becomes the base line for a further small rise until confidence establishes a rush, so a change of attitude is established step by step until it becomes a trend and a flood. Today it is hard to imagine that there was a time when slavery was looked upon as a matter of routine by Christian governments and Christian gentlemen and even quasi-religious bodies like the Order of St. John of Jerusalem.

Change by provocation

Something happens and after it has happened our thinking is never quite the same again. In the process known as lateral thinking great use is made of provocation. A deliberately provocative statement is made: for example that taxi drivers need not know their way around London. At first sight this seems ridiculous. But as a provocation it serves to jerk us out of our usual way of looking at taxis. For example the very low number of taxis in London (much lower than Moscow and very much lower than New York) is partly due to the tough route-knowledge exam which taxi-drivers have to pass in order to get a licence. The studying for this exam often takes six months of exploring the streets on a motor-cycle. The provocation leads us directly to the concept of a two-tier taxi system. The existing tier would remain as it is and would be used by visitors and people from out of town. The new tier would consist of drivers who did not know their way around and would be used only by Londoners who could direct the driver. The taxis would be distinguished in colour and the drivers would, in time, learn their way about anyway. In science a provocative hypothesis can be most useful in getting us to look at something in a new way. Much of art is provocative in this sense. It is not meant to be an accurate descriptive statement but to provoke us into insights, realisations and new ideas.

Change by design

We are always a little wary of change by design since it implies a design that fits the values and considerations of the designer but not necessarily of anyone else. The high-rise apartment blocks built around London some years ago seemed an excellent idea in terms of cost of building and density of housing. But they are now acknowledged to be a disaster because the families living in them are far too isolated from each other: children cannot go out to play and the anonymity leads to vandalism. We would be worried that a designed future would leave out human values or could not take into account the possible changes in needs, preferences and circumstances. Of course there are good designs and bad designs just as there are good architects and bad architects. There are also fixed designs, and flexible designs that allow for adjustment and improvement.

Change through creating institutions

An area of change is perceived and a body is set up to deal with that area. In time this body acquires its own power – or loses it – and change is effected. The setting up of trades unions in the United Kingdom was such a change through institutionalisation. The European Common Market is another example. The purpose of setting up the institution in the first place may not have been to encourage change. On the contrary, it may have been to defuse the situation – to make a gesture of showing that something was being done with the intention that this would avoid the need for real change. Once such an institution was in place then any further protests could be shunted off to that institution. Sometimes, however, such institutions set up as substitutes for genuine change can become foci for change in their own right.

Change through creating alternative tracks

This is change through by-pass. Instead of trying to change the whole system you create a by-pass which leaves the system intact. If the by-pass thrives and attracts more and more traffic then it becomes established and the change has been effected. Freddie Laker created such a by-pass with his low fares to New York from London. It proved such a success that within a short time most major scheduled services were offering special low fares. As an agent of change his by-pass proved most effective. In seeking to establish 'thinking' as a general skills subject in schools I have used the same method. Set up a practical way for teaching thinking as a skill and make it available to schools. If the schools find it of use then eventually it will become established. To date several thousand schools are using the method. It would have been very difficult to attempt a direct change through complaint or exhortation at a central level.

Change through persuasion or exhortation

Salesmanship, argument, persuasion and exhortation are all ways of trying to get someone else to change his view of things. The purpose is to develop insight so that suddenly the listener will see the logic of your argument. The difficulty is to know when persuasion or advertising becomes manipulation, which is then change through coercion. Subliminal advertising is manipulation but salesmanship is not. Then there is the problem of the slanting of information. If you slant your information or select it then you are manipulating the response. Fortunately change through these methods is relatively inefficient. We would probably be unable to tolerate it if it became too effective.

Change through awareness

If you do succeed in seeing something differently then your behaviour may change as a result. The consciousness of pollution and the effect of the Club of Rome's book *Limits to*

Growth were good examples of this. Freudian psychoanalysis is based on change through awareness. That is the sort of change I shall be attempting throughout this book. If we can become aware of the structures and concepts that restrict our evolution then we may be able to adapt more easily to complex circumstances. An idea may have an organising power, an attention power, a value power or an awareness power.

Change through review

In business there is a fashion for what is called 'zero-based budgeting'. Normally at budget time each department puts in a budget both for its on-going activity and to cover new developments. The budgets get trimmed but they get passed in the end. In zero-based budgeting there is no assumption that on-going departments or activities need to go on existing. That is why there is a zero-base. Nothing is taken for granted. Each activity and each department has to justify its existence from scratch – as if it was being set up for the first time. We can do the same with some of the concepts and structures in society. Instead of taking them for granted we can look at them and see if they continue to justify their existence. It may be that some of them are restricting our development and standing in the way of a positive future.

3 THINKING HABITS

There is not much the matter with our intelligence. There is a great deal wrong with our thinking habits and style – in fact with our thinking culture in general. There is a big difference between wisdom and cleverness. In camera terms cleverness is a sharp focus and wisdom is a wide angle lens. We can measure and note cleverness so we promote it. We cannot measure wisdom so we ignore it. We can measure intelligence or see its manifestation in ordinary school work so we promote it. We cannot easily measure thinking skill so we ignore it and assume that thinking skill is but intelligence in action. It is nothing of the sort. Many highly intelligent people are poor thinkers. Many people of average intelligence are skilled thinkers. The power of a car is separate from the way the car is driven.

There is a good reason behind our appallingly inadequate thinking methods. These were developed by the scholastic philosophers of the Middle Ages for a particular purpose. That purpose was the defence of an articulated theology that had been constructed with words and was vaguely related to the teachings of Christ as turned into an imperial religion. The theology had to be kept intact and pure. Above all it had to be defended against the heresies that were forever springing up. Paradoxically many of these heresies were in fact created by the elaborate wordplay of the constructed theology. So the clergy were elaborately trained in disputation and argument. At the university of Salamanca the training took fourteen years – of listening. The style of thinking was directly concerned with so-called logical deduction. Both sides accepted basic concepts and then argument was joined to see whether obtained conclusions were consistent with the premises or not. This is a highly artificial form of thinking specifically designed for a very tight purpose. In fact the style of thinking was based on the Hellenic style of thinking in general, and Aristotle in particular, honed and armed by the brilliantly clear mind of St. Thomas Aquinas who provided the Church with a thinking method that has lasted until today.

This particular thinking method of the Church set the thinking culture of society because for many centuries all education and universities and thinking were indeed in the hands of the Church. Most of the famous universities of Europe were originally Church institutions. So the thinking culture was handed down. Even the French philosopher Descartes had to spend his early thinking years being trained in this style of thinking. Since the Church thinking was based on Hellenic thinking and since the Renaissance introduced to the barbaric world the beauty of Hellenic thinking and the classics, the idiom was reinforced for even those who opposed the Church used its style of thought. To this day our style of thinking is almost totally dominated by that idiom. We take it so much for granted because we do not realise that it is but one idiom of thinking.

Chinese science and technology which were very advanced in their early days came to a stop because the Chinese never developed the concept of an hypothesis. The Greeks were appallingly cumbersome mathematicians because they never developed the concept of the zero (and a suitable notation). Our own social development has been, to my mind, severely retarded because we could not escape from the idiom of disputation and dialectic.

The negative mind

Any system that is defending itself against alteration has no choice but to be negative. Since no alteration is allowed all suggested alteration must be shown to be false.

In general terms it is very much easier to be negative than to be constructive. Any person is able to visit an art gallery and sneer at the exhibited work and yet be totally unable to paint anything himself.

Negativity is the sole activity open to a mediocre mind. A mind that is, itself, unable to create, can only display its talents through criticism of others.

A critic setting out to review a play has a need to fill his column and write something interesting. He is unlikely to be able to do this in praising the play, for his piece will be bland and sound sycophantic or at least fulsome. But in the exercise of an attack he can be brilliant and even witty.

A negative approach is easy because it is always possible to compare what is seen against a model that one chooses for oneself. An ornate piece of furniture is seen as fussy, vulgar and over-elaborate because the chosen model is simple. But if the piece of furniture had been simple then the chosen model would have been more ornate and the piece would have been condemned as stark or plain or utilitarian. No one is ever at a loss for criticism if he is so minded.

Criticising something makes us feel superior. We are as good as the creator and better since we can find fault with the created object. Adulation puts us on a lower level since we are in the posture of adoration and are seen to be a follower.

The sneer is easy and requires no back-up and no justification. It is extraordinary that we can readily accept as sneers such words as do-gooder, pious, intellectual, literary, populariser, workaholic, sober and middle-class.

Malicious gossip is more interesting than tittle-tattle. Attack is more interesting reading than a mere account. Investigative journalism is more interesting than description. A fight is more interesting than a parade.

Having something to oppose gives direction and meaning to life and to action and to thinking. Revolutions would never have succeeded without a hatred of the bourgeoisie or of capitalists. Missions need focus and hatred is the surest way to provide this.

In discussing politics with his friends a man waxes more eloquent and more interesting when attacking the notions of the opposite party to his own than when in praise of his own side. In elections we tend to vote against the other party rather than for our own.

By definition envy is a negative emotion. I suppose the converse is hero-worship which is as positive without reason as envy is negative without reason.

None of the above examples of the negative mind are exclusively to do with the style of thinking developed by the medieval schoolmen. They are more examples of a negative attitude which is then followed by thinking appropriate to that attitude.

The critical intelligence

It is often claimed that the main purpose of education is to develop the critical intelligence. We equip our children with hatchets, not with the seeds of positive contribution. We have traditionally put a higher emphasis on the critical intelligence than on the creative intelligence. We hope that the exercise of critical intelligence will prevent the making of mistakes and help us to resist the blandishments of charismatic nonsense.

Destruction of an idea provides instant achievement. The destruction is an end in itself. There is little achievement to be had in supporting an idea because it takes time for the idea to be shown to work and the achievement is someone else's anyway. But destruction is personal, immediate and final.

If something is ninety-per-cent worthwhile and ten-per-cent wrong we focus our attention on that ten per cent and ignore the rest. It could be supposed that by focusing on that ten per cent the critic was seeking to bring it up to the standard of the rest. But in practice the attitude is rather different. The suggestion is that the criticised ten per cent is only a sample of the whole thing and if this can be shown to be weak then the whole thing collapses. After all you only need one leak to sink a boat. Far too many reviews are niggling, nit-picking and petty-minded. One reviewer even complained that the binding of his copy was faulty and the centre pages fell out.

We seek to improve designs by criticising the faults and trying to improve them. We seek to improve society by indicating the shortcomings and demanding their redress. However, removing the faults in a stage-coach may produce a perfect stage-coach but is most unlikely to produce the first motor car.

Very often a design will be improved not by picking out the faults but by challenging the features which seem beyond criticism and asking for an improvement in them. We should not only focus our attention on what is wrong. There are greater benefits to be obtained from attention to what is just adequate. Or we might even adopt the improvement policy of focusing on the strongest features and asking for their further development. Criticism alone is a poor route to design improvement – yet it is one we habitually use.

As soon as we spot a thesis or hypothesis we immediately search around for an example which refutes the thesis. According to Sir Karl Popper the sole function of an hypothesis is to invite refutation because from the refutation will arise a better hypothesis. Clearly a single refutation will destroy the certainty of an hypothesis. A claim that all swans are white will be refuted by the first spotting of a black swan whereas to prove the hypothesis you would have to examine every single swan. There is a grave danger in this attitude. It excludes the provocative hypothesis, the function of which is to stimulate further exploration from which a better hypothesis will emerge. It also restricts us to absolute hypotheses rather than statistical ones and in some fields this can hold up progress. What we require from an hypothesis is a usable scan of predictions.

If we cannot prove that violence on television encourages violent behaviour in the viewers then we must not try to interfere with the programme content. It is not enough that an accumulation of evidence seems to show this because each experiment can be shown to be imperfect in some sense. I believe that the school curriculum is crowded with subjects that are only of use for the examinations and are of little use later in life. This is to the exclusion of more important subjects – like the development of thinking skills. But it would be impossible to prove that these subjects are harmful because they are not. So since they are beyond criticism they are beyond alteration. A consequence of the critical intelligence is that anything which can survive the critical intelligence is thereby validated or protected.

The adversary system

This arises directly from the disputations of the medieval schoolmen and the Hellenic dialogue. It is the basis of debate and politics and dialectics. The basic principle is that a situation allows just two mutually exclusive hypotheses. If you succeed in proving one of them wrong then you have proved the other right. The trouble is that there are very few situations which allow of only two, exclusive, hypotheses. In practice there may be more than two hypotheses. Or they may not be mutually exclusive so proving one wrong does not prove the other right. In politics destruction of the other person's policy is in no way proof of the validity of yours.

If all you had to do to prove the validity of your argument was to prove wrong the holder of an opposing argument, then the best proof would be to find a fool who supported the other argument.

If you find a weakness in the other man's argument this does not prove the falsity of his conclusion. It merely means that his conclusion is as yet unproven.

It is all too easy in dialectic argument to take the other argument to an extreme – creating what is called a straw man – and then to attack this extreme.

All too often we use debate as a sort of intellectual jousting. If one politician can better another in a debate, the offered conclusion is that he is intellectually superior. This does not follow. He may have been superior on this occasion or, indeed, he may always be superior in the exercise of critical faculties but may be inferior in the exercise of judgement or in creative ability.

There is much of value in debate because the method forces us to focus on the issue and tease out the implications and consequences. But the method often forces the opposing views too far apart, denying them any agreed area of overlap. A valid argument may be lost over a debating point. Each side concentrates its efforts on destructive criticism instead of seeking to develop the most positive aspects both of its own notion and also that of its opponent. There is no constructive cooperation. If an idea occurs to one debater that would strengthen his opponent's case then this idea is suppressed. There is a great deal of wasted intellectual effort and what decides the issue is not the worth of the idea but the debating skill of the proponent. It is also the case that the system is asymmetric insofar as it is usually much more difficult to show why a new suggestion is worthwhile than to show why it will not work. A new idea must often be judged within a new framework but the debate is always carried out within the old framework. We know that all developments in art – and most in science – have been initially condemned when judged in the old framework.

The system that was designed for debating theologians is grossly inadequate to deal in a constructive and positive way with the problems of today. Nor is designing a more positive system difficult – once we have freed ourselves from the tyranny of this habit. In a political system it is difficult to believe that all the wisdom is on one side and that the other side has no contribution to make. The purpose of a court of law is, presumably, to establish innocence or guilt rather than the relative debating skills of two lawyers.

The positive mind

In practical terms it may be argued that for one hundred people to each have an idea would lead to utter chaos and that it must be better for one person to have an idea and the other ninety-nine to improve that idea by criticism. The answer is that with a positive attitude of mind the hundred could between them develop one strong idea by each contributing to its improvement. Alternatively there could be one hundred ideas in the first place and then the best would be chosen and used. One of the strong points of Japanese technology is that the Japanese are positive about the development of ideas. In the United Kingdom on the other hand there is very often the 'not invented here' attitude which means a negative and destructive response to an idea from elsewhere or someone else.

The positive attitude does not mean that every idea has to be treated as wonderful. It means a positive exploration of an idea to discover and show up whatever good features it has. The next step might be to find the weaknesses in order to avoid or strengthen them, rather than using them as a means for rejecting the idea. Finally the fully developed idea may not be used because there is a better one or because – good though it may be – it is not suitable. Too often we feel we have to start rejecting an idea at the beginning because we know that at the end we are not going to be able to act upon it. There is nothing wrong with being positive about an idea and showing, honestly, at the end why it is not possible to adopt it.

With regard to the general negative attitude of mind, perhaps society ought to turn on this attitude its own powerful weapon of the sneer. Perhaps the ease of being negative should be emphasised. Perhaps we should dethrone the critical intelligence from its long domination of our intellectual culture and replace it with the constructive intelligence. We can still use constructive criticism for the focusing of attention on weaknesses which might otherwise be overlooked in a positive euphoria. In any case we could demand of a critic that he must first list the positive points before he earns himself the right to be negative. We must train our youngsters to be more positive in attitude. Too much brilliant mental effort is wasted on negativity. Set a mind in a negative direction and it will perform brilliantly. Set a mind in a positive direction and it will perform as brilliantly. In fact the very first thinking-lesson we use in schools is designed to do just this: focus the mind in a positive direction, in a negative direction and in a direction that is loosely called 'interest'.

With regard to our institutions that rely too heavily on the adversary system we can make a conscious effort to design and develop other methods. For example family courts are now making a move away from the adversary system towards cooperative exploration. The Senate Committee method in the United States is a step towards such constructive cooperation. After all many effective organisations in the world are not run on a dialectical method at all. It is by no means the only way. Naturally the method will be most strongly defended by those who are unable to operate their intellectual equipment in any other way, and those who quite fancy their skills of dialectic desolation.

The problem of opposites

This is a very real problem in our thinking style – but a hidden one. It also arises, indirectly, from the thinking habits of the disputatious medieval schoolmen though in this instance the habit was used as much for constructive theology as for heresy-bashing.

If something is bad then it follows that its opposite is good. There are echoes here of the debate: if you prove one thing wrong then the opposite must be right.

Everyone is agreed that bad logic makes for poor thinking. So naturally it must follow that good logic makes for good thinking. This is, of course, complete nonsense. Good logic is one requirement of good thinking but by no means the only one. Water is a requirement of soup but few would accept a bowl of hot water as a satisfactory soup. Perfect logic can only service the perceptions on which it is required to act. If these are inadequate then the faultlessness of the logic will not improve them and will still give a poor answer. No one has ever suggested that the perfect working of a computer can by itself validate its answers. These can be no better than consistent with the input. Hence the term GIGO which means 'Garbage In – Garbage Out'. When Galileo had performed his elementary experiment on gravity showing that bodies of different weight fell at the same speed, his conclusion was logically disproved by the brilliance of the schoolmen logicians who showed that it could not be so. Galileo's results had also been obtained by de Groot but the excellence of the logic still transcended the fact of experiment.

We accept that tyranny is reprehensible and contrary to human dignity. Therefore it must follow that its opposite – namely freedom – is highly desirable. But this does not necessarily follow at all. What may be desirable is the absence of tyranny and not freedom. The importance of this distinction will be considered at length later in the book.

We know that a sloppy work of ill-supported speculation is not much use for the advancement of human knowledge. So the opposite must be true: that a work of exquisite and detailed scholarship is the proper endeavour of the human mind. The result is that scholarship becomes the triumph of form over content. Many brilliant minds are wasted in detailed scholarship over trivial matters that lend themselves to this approach whilst much more important matters are simply neglected because they do not lend themselves to this approach. Too often the result has the thundering significance of nuns' knitting.

We know that a person who has no knowledge is, by definition, an uneducated person. Clearly this must imply that a person with the maximum amount of knowledge must be maximally educated. So education sees its role as imparting the maximum amount of knowledge. Again this is nonsense. Up to a point we may need pure knowledge but beyond that point it may be more important to supplement that knowledge with thinking skills rather than to pile on yet more knowledge.

If we are decided to make capitalism the enemy then it must follow that the opposite of capitalism will lead to a livable utopia. Again this argument by opposites leads us into trouble and shuts our minds to a whole range of alternatives including different sorts of capital and alternatives other than Marxism. Revolutionaries have repeatedly found – to their cost – that the enemy of your enemy is not necessarily your friend.

Of course the argument by opposites works both ways. If something is bad then the opposite is good. And if something is good then the opposite is bad. So if collectivism is good it must follow that individualism is bad – so excluding a society which can work cooperatively and still have space for individuals.

It also follows that if you are in favour of something it must be implied – even if you have not expressed it yourself – that you are against the opposite. For example if I am in favour of lateral thinking then it must follow that I condemn

logical thinking. In fact we need both. Being against the traditional exclusive dominance of logic is not the same as being
against logic.

The problem of amounts

If love is good then more love is better. If information is useful
then more information is more useful. If order and discipline in
society are necessary then more order and discipline will make
for a better society. If cleverness is important in business then
a more dever man will make a better business man. If learning
history is essential then learning even more history can only be
better still. If socialism is good then more socialism is better.
If poverty is a saintly virtue then more poverty indicates even
more virtue. If freedom of the press is a good thing then more
freedom of the press is better. If travel is a good thing then the
farther you travel the better it is.

We use this sort of thinking a good deal and yet the absurdity of it is patent. If salt is a good thing then more salt must be
better. If one leader in a group is good then two leaders must
be better. If four sparking plugs are necessary to make a car
go then eight sparking plugs will make it go better. If protest
is good then more protest is better. Obviously there are many
things which are good up to a point – like salt. Beyond that
point they may become harmful. Government regulation would
seem to be an obvious example. There are other things which
are only good in the required amount – more of them or less of
them is worse.

Creativity is good and more creativity is better, but yet more
creativity may lead to impotent chaos. The point is obvious
but because of our dialectical habits it is very difficult to dem-
onstrate. I can show you that creativity is good by showing
you the dangers of the lack of creativity (stagnation) and by

showing the usefulness of a certain amount of creativity. On the other hand by looking at an excess of creativity you can argue that creativity is bad. So creativity is both bad and good at the same time. Most arguments are of this sort. There is no doubt that in our thinking we have not solved the problem of amounts – mainly because it evades our traditional thinking methods and political habits. How can you argue that socialism is fine up to a point or that capitalism is fine up to a point?

The sneer is a beautiful illustration of our problem with amounts. We can sneer at an excessively literary person, or at someone who is obsessed by work or someone who is blinded by patriotism or at someone who 'does good' not as an exercise in help but for ego importance. The paradox is that we have to 'sneer' because we cannot show these things to be wrong. We start by sneering at the excesses. But who defines an excess? If the excess is unattractive then surely lesser amounts are also unat-tractive. Before long we find that most things which were once regarded as rather important virtues are the subject of a sneer. Obviously the process can be applied to virtually everything: by taking it to its excess and sneering at the excess, then allowing the sneer to edge downwards until it encompasses the whole quality.

Implicit in our problem of amounts is the idea that amount itself makes no difference. There is the story of the man in a hotel who propositioned a girl and offered her $5,000 to go to his room with him. She accepted, but as they were going up in the elevator the man asked if she would come for a mere $10. The girl was furious:

'What do you take me for?' she asked.

'I thought we had established that,' said he, 'and were now haggling over the price.'

With the girl the amount of money made no difference to the principle (from his point of view, not hers) but with other things the actual amount does make a huge difference. But the example does serve to show how the problem arose from a technological point of view. Once the principle was established juggling with amounts does not matter: for the Catholic Church an artificial method of birth control is still condemned whether it is relatively ineffective or highly efficient. Nor do we allow someone to be just a little bit dishonest.

The problem of absolute ideas

The scholastic heritage in our thinking requires absolute ideas, pure classifications and certain hypotheses. All these arise from the Aristotelian base that St. Thomas Aquinas used. Indeed his celebrated revamping of Aristotle's syllogism becomes useless if this is not so. Consider: all capitalists are thieves; he is a capitalist; therefore he is a thief. Obviously the argument would not work at all if the first proposition read: some capitalists are thieves. In order to guide our politics, our emotions and our morals we have developed absolute ideas.

In fact we defend our civilisation by attacking the slightest threat to any of the absolute principles we hold. The slightest suggestion of an infringement of the freedom of the press is met by howls of outrage because it is felt that once the absolute principle is breached then the floodgates are open and all freedom will be lost.

Similarly we have to have the certain hypothesis in science. The hypothesis that all swans are white is destroyed by one instance of a black swan. But the hypothesis that all swans have long necks is certain and therefore usable (of course if it did not have a long neck we would hardly classify it as a swan). Yet it is possible to develop a whole different approach to science – and perhaps one more suited to a systems world – by dealing with hypotheses which work on the 'by and large' basis. For example: 'by and large swans are white'. Naturally we have been unable to make much progress in this promising direction because we remain largely trapped within the old idiom.

It is easy to see why absolute ideas were required by the Greek thinkers. If you were going to play around with words then the only way you could have a conversation was to have absolute concepts – otherwise there could be no meaning or truth (but just poetry). The medieval schoolmen had the same problem but writ much larger because their whole constructed theology required an absolute construction with brick-solid concepts. The 9,187 philosophy teachers in the USA with their 98 philosophy journals have the same problem today.

To be fair, words are but a classification system to make sense of the world around us, of our thinking and of our communication. If we have a box labelled 'red' then it only makes sense to have that box if everything inside is indeed red. In future we can put our hand into that box and without looking draw forth something that is red. If some things are more orangey than red we take them out of that box and create a new box labelled 'orangey' and in that new box everything is orangey.

Innumerable problems arise from this particular thinking style we have chosen. I do not intend to go into all of them here because it would take a book in itself. We can, however, mention the sampling problem. We saw that the hypothesis that all swans are white can be destroyed by the single instance of a black swan. In a parallel way an ardent socialist would regard the single instance of a plutocrat driving past in his Rolls-Royce as an indication that society was still capitalist – since the car refuted the hypothesis that society was socialist. The fact that the car might be the last remaining Rolls-Royce or that if all Rolls-Royce owners had their entire wealth confiscated it would only mean three cigarettes each for everyone else, is quite irrelevant for we are dealing with absolute ideas.

For ease of emotional administration it is obvious that battle-cries, slogans and party labels all have to be absolute. Whatever comes out of the box that bears your party label must be worthwhile and whatever comes out of the other box must be worthless. You cannot have a battle-cry that is against some naughty capitalists but not against the absolute principle of capitalism. You cannot have a battle-cry against Russian communism but not against the principle of communism. The medieval schoolmen knew full well that ideologies can only work with absolute ideas. Of course this can lead to a certain amount of trouble as illustrated by the remark a young child made to her teacher:

'Can God do everything?'

'Yes, child, he is all powerful so he can do everything.'

'In that case can God make a stone so heavy that God cannot lift it?'

Quite a lot of our political argument is of a similar nature.

The problem of intermediate labels

Intermediate labels are a sort of currency that make more convenient our mental transactions. They include labels like good, bad, sin, undemocratic, exploitation, Marxist and so on. The principle is perfectly sound. You examine a situation and you slap on the label. Whenever you have to deal with that situation again in the future you do not need to re-examine it in detail, you simply read the label. This saves time and clarifies decisions. The labels themselves are unequivocal: they indicate absolute value. We no longer react to the situation but to the label, just as we treat money as a value in itself and not only in relation to what it can buy.

Obviously the trouble arises at the moment of attachment of the label. The attachment may be loose, it may only refer to one part of the situation or the situation viewed in a particular way or to a particular level of some quality. All the nuances and peculiar circumstances of the initial judgement are lost. Imagine that you have a new cook who does not speak English very well. You indicate the salt jar and show that salt is 'good' for cooking. The meal turns out to be so salty that it is inedible. Clearly what you meant – and took for granted – is that the right amount of salt is good. But once intermediate labels are attached we cannot re-examine on every occasion the basis of the attachment. We just accept it and react to the label.

Reactive and projective thinking

Our educational tradition and our thinking culture have always emphasised reactive thinking. At school a problem is set out for us and we react to the situation and solve the problem. In our critical frame of mind we look at something that is being put forward and we react to it. As problem-solvers we receive the problem and we set out to solve it.

In contrast a projective thinker may only have a starting point and a general direction. He then sets out to do something. It may be an exercise in design or creativity or entrepreneurship or project-development. He has to find his own way and generate his own information. This is not set out for him as it is in a textbook problem at school.

In our teaching of thinking in schools (at the Cognitive Research Trust) we have noticed what might be called the 'Everest' effect with the most gifted children. They are used to being stretched by difficult problems that are put in front of them. These problems are of the reactive type: the children are required to use the information given to arrive at an answer. Just as a mountain stands in front of the climbers and is ready to be climbed so the problem stands in front of the children.

They are good at tackling such problems – and the higher the mountain the more the sense of achievement (hence the term Everest effect). But the same children may be very superficial and weak at tackling quite simple problems where the information is not given but where they have to exercise a projective think-ing faculty which they have not developed. In an examination we set to test General Thinking Skills in schools we found that many good academic thinkers were poor projective thinkers. They could react to a given situation but they could not create for themselves the situation in which to make decisions or take action. Such activities as the assessment of priorities, generating ideas, selecting alternatives, guessing and strategy are all part of projective thinking but not part of reactive thinking. The result is that many of our best brains are locked up in a limited think-ing idiom through this early diversion of their talent towards reactive thinking and away from projective thinking. Projective thinking is also constructive thinking.

Our management training schools fall into the same trap. We train managers to be problem-solvers rather than opportunity-finders. We train them to run an organisation smoothly and to cope with the problems that arise from time to time. They are to be car mechanics not car designers. We train managers and not entrepreneurs. We train administrators and not system architects. How then are the systems to change and improve? By correction of faults, by reaction to protest and through the evolutionary pressure of circumstances. This is a very poor route of improve-ment when contrasted with positive design.

The clever person is the reactive thinker: he can solve brain teasers and play chess well and will probably pass the civil service exam. He will write pungent criticisms and perceptive reviews. He will generate his political momentum through following one ideology or opposing another. The wise person is the projective thinker. He will build situations in his mind. He will enlarge his perceptions and alter his perceptions. He will be an entrepreneur, a designer, a creator and a leader. The wise person does not always have to be active but he does bring to a situation much more than is immediately provided by it.

The problem of foresight

This problem arises directly from our emphasis on reactive thinking. There is the story about the man who jumped off the roof of a skyscraper. As he passed the tenth floor window he was heard to mutter: 'So far so good'. If a future disaster is not within our perception as a tangible problem at the moment then we cannot react to it. The problem with criminals is that they do not perceive that they are going to get caught so the severity of the punishment is not a deterrent. An injured hunter who is living off the food in his deep-freeze looks at the food in front of him and enjoys eating it. What happens when the deep-freeze is empty lies in the future and he cannot react to that. In any case anything might happen before that: his injury might improve or someone might stop by and notice his predicament.

Banks arrange loans to Third World countries and when the debts fall due the banks re-schedule them in order not to lose the money since the country is unable to repay it. The amount of debt goes on accumulating and the banks know that the accumulation cannot last for ever but for the moment they are making profits. In the heady days of the American stock-market boom investors bought shares which were intrinsically worthless because they knew they would rise in price and could be sold at a profit. They knew that one day the bubble would burst and that was not today.

Politicians are constrained, by the nature of the system, to short-term views and moment to moment political expediency. They may know the future benefits of some temporarily unpopular policy but the electors see only the immediate effect. We react to what is in front of us.

Just as we find it difficult to react to future problems so we find it difficult to react to future benefits. Religion alone has been able to make future benefits tangible enough at the moment to be reacted to (through a process of disciplined masochism).

General uncertainty, speed of change, inflation and many other factors make us unwilling to predict the future or to react to it. But the basic problem remains our emphasis on reactive thinking. In school we put the emphasis on sorting things out, not on perception. We assume that the world is going to package its problems as neatly as the compilers of school textbooks. And because it does not we search for slogans and labels to provide the ingredients for our reactive thinking.

In the thinking lessons that the Cognitive Research Trust is introducing into the school curriculum the emphasis is not on reactive thinking, not on sorting out given information and not on problem-solving. It is on the development of perceptual skills, on projective thinking, and on wisdom rather than cleverness.

A business manager may be content when things are going smoothly. There is no need to alter anything because there is no immediate problem to be solved. It may be that the market – as with shipbuilding – is quietly slipping away from him but until he perceives that in a tangible way, there is nothing he can react to. We never see any need for altering things that are running smoothly. There are no problems so why should we create some. The projective thinker would not sit and wait for problems. He would look at the strengths of what was being done and try to build on them. He would continually be trying to improve the methods, simplifying them and making them more effective. He would not be content just to run the machine as it was and to wait for problems to arise so he could apply his reactive thinking. In government and in administration of every kind we suffer too much from thinkers who have been trained only to be reactive. The projective leader leads into the future; the reactive leader backs into the future relying on drift and crisis management.

The problem of information

This is also part of our habit of reactive thinking. We spend far too much of our intellectual effort on history. Some of this is justified because history is the only laboratory in which we can watch the interaction of human nature with events. We can certainly learn from history but our perception can also be frozen by an historical perspective that no longer applies. The real reason we are so obsessed with history is that it provides the ideal environment for our reactive thinking style. History is there – we can react to the information. Nor are we going to run out of information. More history is created every day. More detail of history is created every day by the work of other historians. So we have a feast of information to react to. We can isolate ourselves with the information and do our own thinking. There are no messy experiments to be done, no awkward sociological observations, no risky business investments. By now there are enough historians to ensure that history will maintain its dominant position in our intellectual culture. The major question can never be asked: do we study the past just because it is there or in order to help us cope with the present and the future? I have no doubt in my mind what the answer is. We climb Everest just because it is there – in the process we might generate some useful information about oxygen equipment and human endurance.

Again there is nothing wrong with the study of history but too many brilliant minds are locked into this prison and hence locked out of other contributions to society. Too much of our intellectual capital and university facilities is devoted to what is, intellectually speaking, an unproductive investment.

In administration we see a parallel problem. Collect all the information that is there to be collected. After all the process only involves designing a form and making it mandatory for every business to complete the form. In the army there is a saying: 'If it moves salute it and if it does not move paint it white.' In govern-ment administration there seems to be an equivalent saying: 'If it can be counted ask for it, if it can be productive regulate it.' The worry is that the computer will simply be used to make these demands for information even easier by reducing the storage and sorting load.

We know that the availability of the computer in science has done a certain disservice. The careful design of experiments and the generation of provocative hypotheses have been replaced by the idiom of: 'Measure everything in sight, feed it into the computer, carry out a multivariate analysis and at the end you have a definite answer that will justify your next research grant.' In the old method you may have laboured for years and got nowhere. Today you are sure of a computer print-out. And that is good enough for the research administrators who are, after all, administrators and like to see a paper output. The big breakthroughs and conceptualisations that alter the universe of consideration are most unlikely to arise from the new method. Moreover the scientists who might have made those leaps can no longer compete for funds or employment with the number-crunchers. Again, there is nothing wrong with the method but there is a wastage of minds and a misdirection of effort.

The problem of truth, analysis and meaning

Imagine a group of skilled chess-players who played amongst themselves and wrote important observations on the game of chess and critiques of each other's play. Imagine that these players were so advanced that their play no longer had any connection with the ordinary domestic chess-player. Moreover they had invented certain special rules which were known only to themselves. Matters which seemed of the utmost inten-sity and importance to certain groups of these players were incomprehensible and of no importance to anyone else. Imagine that the sheer intellectual skill exercised in this pursuit was of the highest order and could in no way be criticised. When you have completed such imaginings you may have a picture of the state of philosophy today: an in-game played by clever players for their own ends or rather for the game's own end. Through no fault of their own they are entrapped.

The idiom is one of analysis, and more analysis and comment upon analysis and comment upon comment. There are elaborate theories of logical structure – based on some chunk of discourse – refutations, counter-examples and laser-like arguments. All within the rules of the philosophical game.

If it is not that then we are back to history. I remember seeing an advertisement for a university post that required a philosopher who was 'an expert in Kant' and thinking how tragic that small notice was.

From its central position as the very king-pin of human development philosophy has become an etiolated game played in a corner of Academia. Yet the world has a great need for a vigorous philosophy concerned not with preserving ancient traditions and playing petty word-games but with monitoring and developing more effective thinking styles and more useful concepts. The only solution might be to retire all departments of philosophy on double pay and to start again.

We are moving into a complex-system universe and the universe of systems is very different from the static world of the Greeks. The old idiom of analysis does not apply as easily to a system because once you have analysed out the parts you no longer have the operating system – rather like looking for a soul through anatomical dissection. We have not yet developed proper scientific methods for dealing with systems. It is an area to which we need to pay much more attention. The computer will help. But we should not feel that analysing into parts or atomic approach is sufficient for our needs.

In a static universe A is defined by reference to something outside itself – for example a system of coordinates. In a dynamic universe A may be defined by its development into B and B by its development into C and C by its development into A. There is nothing illogical about this circularity. It is also possible to have a practical situation in which A is 'bigger' than B and B is 'bigger' than C and yet C is 'bigger' than A. Again this is quite logical. Our thinking needs to make the same sort of jump that geometry made when it left plane surface Euclidean geometry and moved into the spherical and other geometries. As always it is the change of universe that is important. Once that is made a new logic develops in the new universe. Thinking is at the stage where we have to make this universe-jump.

We may want to move away from box-type classifications to flagpole classifications and the logic that springs from these. We may want to develop 'field' logic and 'pattern' logic. We may fail but we should try. Consider the following absurdity. In lateral thinking one of the provocative techniques is to use a random word to help generate new ideas or solve a problem. Now if the word is truly random then it has no connection with the given problem – and consequently it has as much connection with any other conceivable problem. Similarly any random word has as much connection with the given problem and, consequently, the implied suggestion is that any random word can solve any problem. This is an absurdity totally contrary to any traditional concept of meaning. Yet in practice it works very effectively. And the logic behind its working is very elementary – in the universe of a self-organising information system.

Consider two approaches to the problem of traffic congestion in cities. The first approach is to analyse the problem in detail and measure traffic flows, peak rates, parking spaces and so on. The idea is to find the cause and then try to eliminate it. The second approach would be to say: 'How could we arrange for people to be delighted not to bring their cars into cities?'

That would provide the starting point. In practice the methods overlap. We need both provocation and analysis. With lateral thinking we might say: 'Po a person no longer owned his car when he drove into the city.' From such a provocation might arise concepts that converted private cars into a form of public transport within the city limits.

Our thinking tends to be descriptive, not operative. We aim to describe the true picture. We ask: 'What is this?' rather than, 'What can be done?' In the general system idiom the latter can be as useful.

Summary

In this chapter I have set out to describe some of the deficiencies, inadequacies and even dangers that arise from our traditional thinking system. This system is a particular system that was developed by scholars in the middle ages for a particular purpose. It is rooted in the Hellenic tradition. The system has a lot of advantages and many might claim that the development of civilisation has been due to its application. Others might claim that civilisation, in the social and political sense, might today be much further advanced if we had not been trapped within this system. I do not, myself, take a position on this. A knife is a most useful device but its very structure means that it is also dangerous. We tolerate the danger so long as the usefulness outweighs this. But if the danger grew too strong we might have to ban knives and develop a different system of cutting what we needed.

I have not wished to show that the traditional thinking idiom is bad or dangerous and therefore should be changed for a better one. I have tried to show that it has certain features which lead us to think in a particular way. Where there are abuses of the system we can try to correct them. Where they are structural faults we should be aware of them and seek to compensate for them. In some cases we may have to devise new methods, for example to replace the adversary procedure in some situations.

Above all I wish to suggest we can no longer be complacent and content with our traditional thinking system if we are to enjoy a positive future. We must be realistic about it rather than hysterically defensive. The dangers can be realised. There are positive steps that can be taken immediately and these are either implicit or openly suggested in this chapter. We must be aware of the huge wastage of misdirected intellectual talent that the system has caused and is still causing. We must focus more attention on the importance of thinking and realise that it is much more than exercised intelligence. In some cases there is no easy step to take and we shall simply have to focus deliberate thinking effort on developing new concepts and new thinking styles. There is a very great deal that can be done once we accept that something needs to be done.

There is a crude American expression indicated by the letters CYA which stand for the way you would place your hands in order to protect yourself from a kick in the pants. It means that a person will only take a course of action which he knows will be safe from criticism or attack. Obviously the sort of actions that follow are feeble and restricted. Yet this sort of behaviour arises directly from the misplaced adulation which we bestow on the negative faculties of mind. It would not have been possible to write this book from the cramped position suggested by CYA.

4 ORGANISING METHODS

Just as we have developed methods, styles and habits of thinking so also have we developed habits of organising. On the
whole these are pretty good. You can pick up the telephone
in London and within ten seconds be speaking to a particular
person in Australia. A multi-national company like IBM operates with a high degree of efficiency. Food distribution in the
developed countries is reasonably effective. Looking out over a
large city like London or New York it is possible to marvel that
every habitation is supplied with water that is drinkable and
with a sewage system. Much that we take for granted shows
evidence of powerful organising habits. Yet we can still look at
some of these habits and wonder whether they do not contain
structural inefficiencies.

Selection, qualification and promotion

It may be that our basic concepts of employment, work and
jobs need changing. That aspect will be discussed later. For
the moment we can consider how we attempt to put the right
person into the right job. We have exams at school, on leaving
school and again at university level. But we are not quite
decided whether their purpose is to encourage the pupil to
work, to test the amount of knowledge imbibed or, repeatedly,

to test innate intelligence. It usually turns out that the subject-matter taught has very little to do with the requirements of any job – outside specialised vocational training as in medicine. The idea is that the trained mind with a broad background and a habit of study has a general potential that can be applied to any situation. Unfortunately the selection process, whether by aptitude tests or by multiple choice exam or by traditional essay type exam, depends very heavily on academic ability. Yet for many jobs personality, drive and the ability to get on with people are much more important. We sometimes seek to assess these at a brief interview or with a battery of psychological tests. We make virtually no effort to develop these aspects or to monitor their development at an early age. We operate education as a rather elaborate and drawn out selection process that uses a practical – but largely irrelevant – basis for the selection. If we look at job skills, life skills and culture skills we find that the emphasis is on the latter.

It is already possible to design people-proof jobs that will not depend on the ability of whomsoever may fill them. But it must always be better to design jobs around clusters of abilities and motivations and then to find people who would enjoy such jobs. There is a world of difference between a manager who enjoys managing and one who is only there for the money and the status.

In order to get more money and more status a person often has to be promoted away from the job he enjoys doing and is good at: the scientist away from the laboratory; the teacher away from the classroom; the nurse away from the ward; the sales manager away from his sales team. The natural progression is expected. We could devise alternative systems without too much difficulty.

It may be that it is too much to expect one person to have all the necessary skills for a job. It may be that we shall have to fill some jobs with a team of two: one of them might have the required people-skills and the other the administrative skills.

Perhaps the team could work permanently together as a double act. Many successful enterprises have, behind the scenes, just such a team of entrepreneur and accountant.

We can state Catch-24: the qualities required to reach a position are not the ones required in that position. Or conversely: in order to reach a position a person has to be devoid of the qualities required in that position. In the first instance we can see that a politician may have a great skill for getting elected and fighting elections but no skill for government. In the second instance a chief executive might have to be something of an entrepreneur and risk-taker but such qualities in a middle manager might block promotion. A series of selection gates, each of which is quite appropriate to its own level, may weed out talents which are required at a higher level. In most countries today the most able people probably do not go into politics because although they may possess the required governing skills they do not possess the robustness necessary for political survival.

The pressures of competition mean that most people are considerably over-qualified, from an academic point of view, for the posts they take up. In the US over the period 1976 to 1985 it is estimated that 10.4 million graduates will compete for the 7.7 million jobs for which a degree is normally required. This availability will simply mean that jobs which hitherto did not need a degree qualification will suddenly be found to require one. And so the escalation will continue with a larger and larger fraction of life being taken up with the preliminaries to a selection test.

Pigeonholes and specialists

Knowledge is increasing at an explosive rate and in order to keep up with knowledge in a particular field a specialist is having to specialise in a smaller and smaller area. And yet society needs generalists who can take a broad integrated view. We still have not solved the dilemma of specialists and generalists. What we tend to do is to employ worn out specialists, who can no longer keep up with their field, as generalists. But the general view is itself a speciality that should be treated as such with a background and training in this area.

The problem is that the world does need generalists but at any particular moment it makes more sense to appoint a specialist. This is a particular expression of Catch-23 which will be met again later. Once you have defined the problem or focused on the university department then you are better off with a specialist. A generalist is only a transition state: a house is some time a-building but it is the final house we live in not the state of being built. I see no reason why we should not create a definite profession of generalists rather than regard them as failed specialists.

Nor have we solved the pigeonhole problem. Something that is everyone's business ends up by being no one's business. Departments, faculties, classifications are key elements in our organising method. When I first asked the Schools Council for some funds for field officers to respond to the demand from schools who were taking up the teaching of thinking as a curriculum subject, I was told that it would be difficult for the matter to be considered because whilst there were subject committees for Mathematics, Geography and all the traditional subjects there was no such committee for 'thinking'.

In administration the person who does not fall neatly into one category or who falls into more than one category causes endless complications. When someone wanted to leap a bus across the river Avon in the summer of 1978 the authorities had to grant the bus a temporary licence as a 'pleasure craft' in order to keep their categories clear.

In medicine we have doctors who are fully trained to know everything there is to know about all diseases. Yet the bulk of a doctor's work could be done by a new type of doctor who was trained to deal competently with the five most common calls on a doctor's time (probably cardiovascular troubles including hypertension; depression; peptic ulceration; minor injuries; and chest complaints). The training need last no more than two years at most and could probably be done in one. But the idea would be resisted by the established categories.

Does a government department or university faculty ever vote itself out of existence in recognition of its obsolescence?

Urgent and important

An executive is surrounded by matters that require urgent attention. There are problems to be solved and decisions to be made. He never runs out of urgent things to do because he can always think of other urgent matters that require his attention. If he does not have sufficient urgent matters he can always go into each matter in greater detail, expanding his work to fill the time allotted to it in classic Parkinson's Law fashion. When he is finished with the urgent matters then he can turn his attention to the important ones but – as we have seen – he is never finished with the urgent matters. If your tyre has a puncture you have to deal with it because it is urgent. The matter of deciding where you want to go or the route to take is more important but urgent matters have to take precedence.

An executive is too busy keeping things going and solving urgent problems to have time to look for opportunities. He knows that it is essential to look for opportunities if his business is to survive but it never makes sense to do so at any particular moment. So we come to Catch-23: it is essential that something gets done but it never makes sense to do it at any particular moment. This is in the same general area as 'who will bell the cat?'

There are no vacuums in an executive's time or in his budget. Everything is allocated. In order to try something new he has to displace something else: he has to make time and find the funds. This general problem of innovation applies to most areas. The school curriculum has no gaps. In order to try something new the school has to displace effort and time from something else. But why divert effort that is usefully employed to something that is at best speculative? This is a basic weakness in our organising for innovation and it cannot be overcome by exhortation. We need a structure change that allows a discretionary budget of time and money that is earmarked for innovatory spending.

Change and innovation

We know from experience that change will happen anyway. The eccentric inventor will fight his way through. If the mousetrap is worthwhile, the world will beat a path to the door of the inventor. We spend quite a lot of money on research and most organisations have R & D departments. But research is not the same as change or innovation. We never set up, within organisations, formal departments of change. We dare not do so because that would imply that we were not satisfied with the perfection of the status quo.

In fact in most organisations innovation is discouraged by the structure. A failed innovation constitutes a bad mistake that blights the subsequent career of whoever was foolish enough to attempt it. Even if the innovation succeeds the innovator runs the risk of being labelled an 'ideas man' and hence not sound enough to run a department.

We believe that evolution should be gradual, unconscious and forced upon us. Anything else is too risky and liable to lead to mistakes and confusion. Yet the proper management of change does not mean jumping at every new fad or overloading an organisation with change. Change can be managed sensibly like anything else. But we must regard it as an integral part of an organisation's function, not as something that is forced upon it.

A major defect is a lack of suitable test-beds. There are a few innovations that can be tested in a laboratory or a computer simulation. A very few (in the field of finance or cost saving) can even be proved with a pencil and paper. But most innovations – and especially those involving people and methods – need to be tried out. Unfortunately even the special circumstance and excitement of trying them out can give false results (the well-known Hawthorne effect) and traditional test-bed areas (like the Tyne-Tees television area for new product testing) soon become atypical. The problem is a major one because it is unrealistic to expect an organisation to embark on a costly change which might turn out to be a disaster. We need to spend a lot more thinking on the development of test-bed structures. For example how could a government try out the suitability of a new type of taxation? Perhaps a few people would have to be given the option of paying taxes in a novel way. No doubt this would cause political trouble. For example a corporation might be asked to pay taxes in proportion to its total wages bill without person-by-person allocation.

Rather than wait for change to happen spontaneously and sporadically perhaps we ought to make more effort to focus attention on areas that need improvement. We could prepare and fund innovation briefs and tenders could be invited for the assignment. The direction of change – for example towards simplicity or greater human value – can be clearly defined.

Projects, developments and new ideas

We need to pay a great deal more attention to the handling of new ideas. There are problems. For example we could look at the 'take-off' effect and the 'wonder-woman' effect.

A plane taxies along the runway picking up enough speed to take off. Until take-off actually occurs the plane is a danger to itself and to its surroundings. Many schemes may be fine once they have reached a critical size or acquired momentum or been in operation long enough. But before that 'take-off' point is reached they may be highly dangerous. For example a more lenient attitude towards criminals might be effective in the long run but in the meantime it could cause trouble. A changeover from direct taxation to indirect taxation might be beneficial in the long run but the immediate rise in prices might be inflationary.

In planning any change we need to look not only at the final result but at the transition stage. Indeed the transition stage is even more important than the final result for unless the transition stage is possible the final result is merely hypothetical. We so often plan for utopias but forget to specify the bus that is going to get us there. This important matter of the transition stage will be discussed at greater length later in the book.

The wonder-woman effect refers to idealised schemes that are attractive in themselves but will only work if the people involved in them are skilled, perceptive, dedicated, compassionate and exceptional. It seems, for example, that progressive teaching methods work better than the traditional ones – provided they are used by good teachers. Bad, or uninterested, teachers achieve better results with traditional methods. The dilemma is a real one: is innovation withheld because some people are incapable of carrying it through or is it put through in the knowledge that some will be better off and some worse off? In theory the answer is to design as much for use as for effect.

Another difficulty is that of intended effect. For example in classic Keynesian theory if there is a recession then the government 'primes' the pump by increasing public work expenditure and reducing tax in an effort to encourage consumption by putting more money into the consumer pocket. This part works well enough but, unfortunately, the consumer still has the final say. He may choose to save the money and we know that in the recent bout of inflation and increasing unemployment saving rates in countries like Australia increased considerably. Or he may choose to spend it not on locally manufactured goods but on imports and so the rise in consuming power simply sucks in more imports and does not reflate the economy.

There are also schemes which work well provided everyone else plays the game and does the same thing. Disarmament is an obvious example. Similarly, if one union restricts its wage claim and others do not then it is likely to be left behind in a position from which it can never catch up.

A major problem is that of foreseeing the effect of action which is temporarily beneficial but the long term effects of which are not clear. The Laffer curve in taxation is one example. Squeezing the productive sector of the economy may work very well right up to the point where it fails and failure may take a very long time to be reversed. If investment has been discouraged then low productivity produces low profits and high prices and the money and will to invest are not there. It may be that a particular course of action is not in itself harmful but brings about a state of vulnerability. For example a single source supplier for an industry is not in itself harmful – in fact it is probably more efficient – but it increases vulnerability.

In general we need much more thorough systems thinking rather than ad hoc solutions and ad hoc rescue attempts when they go wrong. The shift is needed from the concept that we are fundamentally in a stable world in which things need adjustment now and then, to the concept that we are in a changing world and that the design of ideas and action should be appropriate to that.

The problem of continuity

We can look at several different sorts of continuity. At any moment in history we strive to make the best of what is available at the time. So we may set up structures which are useful at the time but outrun their usefulness and become obsolete and restrictive later. We rarely build-in evolutionary processes and we have no method of making thriving institutions obsolete. For that matter we have no method of removing obsolete laws unless a time limit has been put on them in the first place. In many cases the cost of change is enormous since it consists in unlocking the interlocking of the various ingredients.

Then there is the continuity of momentum like a billiard ball rolling in a certain direction. There is no structural bar to change – as there was in the interlocking situation – only the momentum of habit. There is need to apply some pressure and make a change effort but the change itself is surprisingly easy. I suspect changes in our work habits would be like this.

There is another type of continuity like a rat running down a drain-pipe. The rat is constantly looking for an avenue of escape. In this sort of continuity there is pressure for change but it awaits the development of an avenue or concept that allows a new direction. There is no resistance to change but change will not take place until the path is offered. To some extent changes in education might be of this sort although there is a considerable degree of interlocking continuity in this area. The Open University in the UK is a good example of this sort of avenue opening. Change through 'by-pass' falls into the same general area: instead of unlocking and altering the main structure, set up a new by-pass channel.

In many situations the problem of the 'apostolic succession' is important. The first pope and the first bishops in the Catholic Church were the apostles and since they then appointed the next lot, who in turn appointed the next lot, the succession was maintained. In many organisations the new candidates are selected and appointed by the existing hierarchy. This is of excellent value where the idiom is dynamic and effective but it is, equally, harmful where the idiom is obsolete. Where an organisation is crying out for a new type of man the apostolic succession ensures that he will not be appointed.

The 'ratchet-effect' refers especially to social expectations. A new service is very quickly taken for granted and becomes the baseline from which further progress is expected. A wheel with a ratchet attached can only move forward not backward. No matter how small the forward movement may be at any moment it is preserved by the ratchet. Once satisfied, desires and expectations are no longer desirable but routine and necessary. In other words they have lost their value in the eyes of those who wanted them but their cost remains exactly the same as before to those providing them. The ratchet effect is the opposite of zero-base budgeting in which each item has to be justified anew or dropped. Measures, like the Employment Acts in the UK, that protect each stage of development inevitably give rise to the ratchet effect since flexibility is lost. We need to devise structures that allow flexibility in both directions. It is not easy because many structures in society act as 'rectifiers' in the electronic sense: they change any fluctuation into an upward one. A rise in wages leads to an increase in commitments and hire-purchase undertakings all of which cannot be abandoned. It is in the area of complexity that the ratchet effect is most dangerous. Things become more and more complex with each little addition (as with the tax laws) and there is little attempt to make them more simple. The reason is that simplification means alteration and even the smallest alteration puts at a disadvantage someone who is playing the system exactly as it is. We need, however, to make simplification a direct responsibility of the change department that was mentioned earlier. It is incredible that no one actually has any responsibility for making things simpler.

The problem of distribution

We badly need new thinking here. Whether it is jobs and houses or food stores and starving people, we face two fundamental problems: there is not enough to go round so who gets it; what is needed and who needs it are in different places. The market economy method uses demand and supply linked by freely fluctuating price as the distribution mechanism: it will be considered later. Then there is central planning and direction and finally there is an assisted market economy which uses regulation and subsidies to supplement price-induced flows.

Where there is not enough to go round we have several options of distribution. The price method has been mentioned. There is a privilege method whereby some people – as with party officials in the USSR – get access to goods before others. The privilege may be historic or it may be conferred; or it may be earned: for example when war veterans have privileged access to education. There is straightforward rationing or rationing by time and convenience. In the Soviet Union some consumer goods are in such short supply that there seems to be deliberate rationing by time: you queue up to look at the goods; then queue up again to pay for them; then queue up for a third time to exchange your cash receipt for the items. We do not make too much use of the lottery system although it would appear to offer some social advantages in terms of political acceptability – but not in terms of efficiency. Rationing by need or distributing where it will do most good are areas that need a great deal more attention.

One of the great structural problems is dealing with those who require special treatment. For some reason, be it illness or inadequacy, they are unable to keep up. Should there just be a safety net, should society be held back to decrease the pressure, or should they be treated in a distinct way? In short do such people need crutches in order to operate in the ordinary world or do they need a world in which there are no stairs? In business there is the classic 80/20 situation in which what takes up 80 per cent of the time actually produces only 20 per cent of the profits and the other way round. In society a small number of members may take up a large amount of effort and cost. But the purpose of society is not profit. Nevertheless the problem of distribution of cost and effort remains.

With increasing pressure on taxes, in addition to their reaching saturation point it will no longer be open to government to encompass all demands by raising more money. Cost cutting and increased efficiency should make a big difference initially but this will reach a floor. This brings up the problem of priorities and the choice between priorities. Do we have the right structures to choose between priorities? Can we solve the problem just by cutting back all round? Is it good enough for each interest group and government department to jockey for its own priorities? Should £5 million be spent on: a new acute hospital; an old persons' home; a fighter plane; a local government administration hall; a new roadway segment; a sports centre; cancer research; job protection in an ailing industry; airport enlargement? Who is to decide, on what basis and through what structures? Are lobbying and mobilised protest better than central planning? Should there be fixed ratios of expenditure with each department required to work within its own envelope? This is not easy because in an area like education about 80 per cent of its costs are people costs and if wages rise then its allocation may need to rise if the non-people expenditure is not to be squeezed out. Departments that can shed people in favour of hardware would benefit.

Problems arising from communication

The sheer effectiveness of our communications systems creates problems. Within moments all banks can think the same way and transfer money, so creating wild swings in the foreign exchange market. Any indication of mood change somewhere is so widely reported that it can become an investment stampede or panic. Everyone knows that things will move quickly so action has to be taken as quickly as possible. The general problem of the self-fulfilling prophecy arises: if enough people think that something is going to happen – for example collapse of the dollar – then that thinking can actually cause it to happen.

Mass communication through television means that every happening and every remark of a politician are instantly communicated. This means that there is a lot of politics of gesture and the right noise. It also means that there is a great deal of what was referred to as CYA: that is to say the avoidance of decisions which can lead to criticism. The existence of television means that politicians have to appear on television and elections are won and lost on profiles and TV personalities.

Issues are simplified and explained in mass-think terms (usually under-rating the intelligence of the viewer) and so the immediate, the concrete and the popular take precedence over the more farsighted and temporarily unpopular policies. Ideas are discussed in the necessarily superficial idiom of television and mass circulation press media. The paradox may be that democracy cannot work now that technology has provided the perfect technical means for it to work as it has always been supposed to work. Perhaps government by the people can only work as an ideal but not as a fact.

Other problems are created by the technology of communication. The telephone and the car break up communities by making it possible for people to have dispersed communities of friends they choose and like. The concept of a local community where you had to accept everyone who was around is lost.

The treatment of risk

Our insurance mechanisms are remarkably effective at dealing with a particular type of risk: the occasional disaster the cost of which is spread amongst all those vulnerable to this type of disaster. We justify profits on the basis of the capital risk involved in ventures. Large organisations and governments can simply absorb the cost of failure through reserves or by distributing it amongst all their other activities.

Perhaps we need to pay rather more attention to the structures available for handling risk. In particular we need to consider the sort of risks that are quite likely to happen rather than the exceptional ones that can be handled by ordinary insurance. Life insurance is insurance against an exceptionally early death and otherwise an organised savings plan for death at a more usual age. Losing a job, getting a divorce, having to move house are all relatively common. From the community's point of view further education is a risk in as much as the money invested on behalf of a person may be wasted. The fluid ratios between investment, benefits, risk and reward need to be considered carefully. We cannot cut down on the reward and yet expect to enjoy the benefits, such as increased employment, of risk taking. Perhaps we could set up concepts and structures where risks as such could be bought either directly or through government guaranteed risk bonds.

We have to consider what happens in a failed venture. Is it like a stillborn child where all is lost, or is it like an unsuccessful fishing trip where the potential remains intact for use on another day? We are probably too inclined to treat venture risks in the former manner. Perhaps we also need a nursery attitude towards ventures with a coddling attitude of tax advantages and management service support.

We can minimise risks by pre-testing and by planning but we should not imagine that we can avoid all risks by never undertaking ventures. In a changing world to do nothing may be the biggest risk of all.

People may be more willing to re-train or change jobs if the risk element is reduced. Moving house to a new district is less of a risk if there is the possibility of returning to the original house if it does not work out. As in trial marriages the argument is that no serious effort will be made if the fall-back position is guaranteed but, conversely, no change at all may be attempted unless the risk is reduced. Guaranteed termination-of-employment payments (not redundancy payments) would ease moving from one job to another – perhaps a forced saving on the part of the worker could be matched by the employer.

The structure of protest

We need to pay more attention to the structure of protest whether it is protest by strike or protest by pressure groups. The effect of the whole structure of the political system will be considered in a later chapter but protest also exists in its own right. Creations such as the Ombudsman are a recognition that systems are not perfect. Can protest be institutionalised without losing its vitality? Perhaps there are people who need a mission and a dedication. Perhaps there are people who need an ego platform in a sort of spiritual entrepreneurship. After all many excellent volunteer organisations work on this basis. The motivation behind a protest has nothing to do with its social validity.

We may have to devise structures which will allow protest its useful function and yet avoid escalating disruption – which will inevitably happen if protest finds it harder and harder to gain attention through the media. Tied in with this general problem is that of the attention paid to minority interests. Can we operate a market economy in attention, or do we run risks with an inflationary price structure? The terrorist hijacking of aircraft is to gain attention, so was the self-immolation of the Czech student who poured petrol over himself. There is a distinction between a consumer movement with a natural constituency (like the campaign for real ale in the UK and the coffee boycott in the USA) and a protest that has first to gain attention in order to gain followers (like the protest at seal hunting). Should we have daily ten-minute protest slots on television just after the news?

Committees, bureaucracies and hierarchies

We know very well that the behaviour of a committee is very different from that of a single decision-maker. It tends to be more balanced and it tends to be more negative. It tends to construct a compromise rather than a bold integral design. It tends to be conservative and repetitive or self-consciously innovative. All these aspects arise from the nature of the structure. We use committees as a protection against dictatorship and decisive mistakes, as a CYA posture. We are not convinced that battles in wartime could be won by committees of generals. We often use committees to make the strategic decisions and then delegate an individual to carry it through and choose the tactics. Perhaps we could reverse that and have individual decisions modified by advisory committees. There is room for new thinking here. Perhaps committees should be hired for the occasion and not be an integral part of the organisation – so separating the judgement element from the vested interest element.

With bureaucracies we need to look at their growth, their purpose, the lines of communication and the responsibility at each level. We badly need to develop a measure of effectiveness corresponding to productivity in an industrial organisation. We need to introduce flexibility and the ability to deal with exceptions. We need to build in motivation and efforts towards change and simplification. Instead of assuming that the purpose of an organisation is to preserve its status quo we should assume that the purpose is to alter its status quo. Suppose we decreed that any civil servant who could eliminate his own job, to the satisfaction of a panel and with the test of time, would be entitled to full pay – as a pension – thereafter. We have the morality of hard work but not the morality of effectiveness. You please God by working hard but not, apparently, by organising your work so that you produce the same effect (or better) by working less hard.

We may need to change our concepts of hierarchy and promotion. There is no reason why authority hierarchy and decision hierarchy should go together. In Japanese industry it is said that decisions are made on the shop-floor and then passed up to the authority hierarchy for proclamation. Is it the person or the position that matters most? Should we create jobs for leaders or expect the job to make leaders out of people who are not?

We need to do a lot of thinking about the overlapping of different hierarchies, for example unions, management, and investors. Should they be integrated or should they operate in a state of dynamic interaction – and if so is the dialectic conflict the only possible state of interaction?

Summary

I have touched in this chapter on a few of the basic structural problems that face society. Later I will deal with more specific areas like politics, education, the market economy and so on. There are many more areas I could have touched on and much more detail I could have gone into. I have not offered easy solutions or suggested changes. In most cases I have simply indicated that there is much thinking to be done or a dilemma to be handled. This is not very helpful or constructive but I do not feel it to be my purpose to offer instant solutions to everything. By thinking around each problem I could certainly come up with suggestions – but so could many other people. Some time that work will have to be done, perhaps by focused groups that are set up specifically to consider these areas that demand thinking. My purpose in the chapter was to show how our future is shaped and sometimes constrained by certain organising habits that we have acquired. Many of these are excellent. Many we consider excellent only because our imagination has not yet thought of something better. Many are imperfect, restrictive or even dangerous. The basic message is that we do need to think about these things and in a positive way. We should not throw up our collective hands and say that they are too complicated to think about or that any designed solutions must inevitably be worse. Above all we should look at the purpose of an organisation not as conservative stability but as dynamic change. Change does not mean the revolutionary swapping of one system for a supposedly better one but building on strengths, changing concepts where necessary, and introducing new concepts in parallel. The combination of constructive thinking habits and something to think about should allow our intelligence to do well for us.

5 LOGIC-BUBBLES AND BUBBLE-LOGIC

The Greeks lacked a suitable mathematical notation and so whilst they were excellent at geometry even simple multiplication was very awkward. With the Roman notation adding up was easy enough because it was a simple tallying system but other types of mathematics were difficult. The Indians invented the marvellous concept of the zero and this passed to the Arabs in about 300 BC. The zero together with the Arabic notation at last allowed mathematics to develop. The Leibniz notation for the calculus was much more convenient than Newton's notation.

We should not overlook the value of notation both in terms of the notation we put on paper and the notation images and concepts we use in our minds. This chapter is concerned with a simple perceptual notation of this sort.

Intelligence and stupidity

Throughout this book I have taken it as axiomatic that people are highly intelligent and that the relative stupidity shown by society is not due to lack of intelligence but – on the contrary – to the exercise of that intelligence. How is it that a series of highly intelligent decisions can add up to something that is unintelligent?

A man uses his hunting knife to amputate his own right hand. That is clearly unintelligent behaviour because quite apart from the pain and danger of bleeding to death he is making work and life very difficult for himself. But it turns out that he did it to free himself from a blazing automobile inside which he was trapped by his hand after an accident. Given that peculiar set of circumstances it was highly intelligent behaviour.

A logic-bubble is the total set of perceived circumstances that logically determine action at any particular moment. In other words we live in the bubble of our perceptions and at any moment we act sensibly and intelligently in a logical manner determined by those perceptions. A unique set of circumstances has a unique action that is determined by them. This is referred to as the polarity of that particular logic-bubble. The notation is very simple and is shown in Figure 1. The surrounding bubble of perceptions is shown as a circle and the polarity of the logical determined action is shown as a stroke across the rim of the circle.

Figure 1

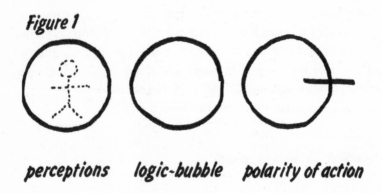

perceptions   logic-bubble   polarity of action

It is important to remember that the bubble does not consist of the actual world around but of a person's perception of that world. Sometimes the two may be similar but at other times there may be differences.

Consider a party in a car looking for a restaurant in which to dine. One of the party remembers that there is a famous restaurant in a certain nearby village so they drive in that direction. Had they but known it there was an even better restaurant in another village and knowledge of this would have led them to take a different direction. Had they been willing to travel further afield then a wider circle of search would have revealed a more distant restaurant and again the direction of action would have been different. The process is illustrated in Figure 2. In each case their action is determined by their perceptual bubble which includes hunger, knowledge of the existence of the restaurants and of their relative value (if there are more than one) and the approximate distance they want to travel.

Figure 2

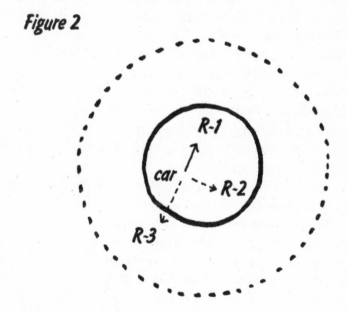

We can talk of selfishness, short-sightedness, limited vision, tunnel vision and self-interest and in a way we will be talking about logic-bubbles, but all these terms have a moral and condemnatory flavour. I wish to emphasise that it is highly intelligent to act in accordance with your logic-bubble. It is only if we consciously accept this that we can move away from exhortation and condemnation.

In the United States there is a move to have tax bands indexed. As incomes rise with inflation the purchasing value of the income remains the same. Nevertheless the income moves into a higher tax band and so more income tax is paid.

The situation is even worse in the UK where the taxation rises much more steeply to the high level of 83 per cent of income. All this is equivalent to a government making a huge increase in income tax but not getting blamed for it because inflation has been responsible. The Federal Reserve Chairman in the USA, G. William Miller, condemned the move towards indexation of the tax bands 'As an insulation from the consequences of inflation – hence making inflation acceptable and lessening the will to fight it'. This is a perfectly logical view within a logic-bubble that contains the electorate, the financial institutions and industry. It could of course be argued that failure to index tax bands provided a huge tax windfall for the government – in excess of that required by inflation – and so made inflation positively attractive to the government which was, after all, in the best position to do something about it.

The Soviet Union is expanding its cargo fleet rapidly and it already has something like 40 per cent of the world fleet. The logic-bubble contains the need to earn hard currency through exporting a service; the low wages of the seamen; possibly some spying activity; possibly the strategic consideration that if they dominate the world cargo fleet other carriers will back out and in time of war the world could be deprived of cargo transport (the Soviets could scuttle their ships if in danger of capture). In the free world an exporter or shipping agent is delighted to use the Soviet vessels because they are very much cheaper than any other vessels. This is perfectly logical within a logic-bubble that relates cost to profits or at least to sales. The British government has a problem because British shipyards have no work and if they closed the increase in unemployment would do their electoral chances no good (and in any case the shipyards are in areas where there is no alternative employment) so the government heavily subsidises the yards to build ships for Poland: ships that are going to compete against the British ships and are indirectly under Soviet control. So everyone is acting perfectly logically within his own logic-bubble.

The British Petroleum company pioneered the production of high class protein from micro-organisms grown on oil waste. The cost of production would eventually be very low when there was volume production and the amounts that could be produced would have made a significant contribution to the world shortage of protein. The logic-bubble is clear enough. But it is said that some of the countries to which the protein was offered had a different logic-bubble. They saw that increased protein might cause an increase in their populations so causing considerable problems and more poverty. They saw that they would be forever tied to the BP supply as a captive market, having to use their precious foreign exchange for this purpose. They declined the offer.

Just as the term logic-bubble refers to the total set of perceptions that at any moment determine action so we can refer to the logic generated by that bubble as 'bubble-logic'.

At a seminar in Toronto I suggested that women's wages ought to be raised so that they were 15 per cent above those for men. To my astonishment the women's-libbers in the audience cheered the suggestion saying that it was about time and no more than women were worth. My own logic-bubble was different: I imagined that if women became much more expensive to employ than men, employers would prefer to employ men (who were in the main the family breadwinners) and so employment could be distributed in a way that benefited families more. I also imagined that the women in the audience would see this at once and denounce the 'trick'. All I can suppose is that their liberation logic-bubble was too strong and too opaque. Perhaps they also felt that since they, themselves, were not going to lose their jobs they would get an extra 15 per cent in their pay packets.

In India families are said to be delighted if a child turns out to be a cripple because his earning power as a beggar is higher than it would have been as a normal child and eventually an adult. One cannot quarrel with the logic-bubble.

In Cambridgeshire a school indicated to the local examination board that it wished to present 'Thinking Skills' as an examination subject. The board replied, quite logically, that this was not possible because an examination board in this subject could not be set up. The school enquired when this might come about and were told that when enough schools were taking it as an examination subject then there would be people from whom to draw an examination board. At each stage one can see the clear logic-bubble.

In the UK the recent Rent Act offered the same protection to tenants in furnished accommodation as had been granted some time previously to those in unfurnished accommodation: the landlord would not be able to turn them out. The logic-bubble of many landlords was as follows: I shall not be able to get rid of the tenants and therefore shall be unable to sell the property to get a capital gain; the rents are very low and much lower than I could get by selling the property and investing the proceeds; in some cases the cost of repairs and maintenance will exceed the rental income; the litigation and hassle involved are not worthwhile. The result was that landlords were not keen to let, did not build or convert for letting, and sold where they could. The amount of property available for letting declined sharply. Already-established tenants benefited but would-be tenants found a shrinking market.

A US reporter from the *New York Times* is sentenced to jail by a court because he refuses to hand over the notes he obtained, confidentially, from a murder suspect. The logic-bubble of the reporter and the *New York Times* who supported him is clear. So is the logic-bubble of the court with its duty to administer justice.

A union leader puts forward a large wage claim. He fears that if he is not militant enough then he will be displaced by others more militant. He knows that if the claim succeeds it will encourage parallel claims from others and this will fuel wage-push inflation. But if he can stay ahead of inflation by keeping wages rising he may conceivably get a real rise in income for his men at the expense of those whose earnings do not keep pace with inflation but who have to pay the higher prices for what they buy. Here the logic-bubble is determined by various factors induding the structure of unions, by his knowledge of those around.him, by his experience of the behaviour of others, by his expectations of the bargaining procedure.

Television companies have to attract high audience ratings in order to attract advertising and charge high rates. They are in a highly competitive situation. They are also run by professionals who know that an average programme with violence is more interesting to viewers than an average programme without violence (the same may not apply to the best programmes but there are too few of these). That is one logic-bubble. Researchers show, and others claim, that TV violence encourages violence in society and contributes to the rapidly rising crime rate.

The problem of clashing self-interests has, of course, been the key problem of society from the beginning. There are a large number of ways in which society has sought to deal with the problem.

Free for all

There is a feeling that as civilisation progresses the framework should become strong enough and the material wealth great enough for everyone to do their own thing. In other words that there is no need at all to align the polarity of the different logic-bubbles – as suggested in Figure 3. It is highly unlikely that this will ever be possible unless we are so disciplined that our logic-bubbles (care for each other, care for the environment) are aligned anyway. As Henry Ford said in his classic phrase: you can choose any colour so long as it is black. Narita airport in Japan is a typical problem. Over 3 million Japanese travel abroad every year. In addition there are visitors to Japan. Business travel both by Japanese executives and by buyers feeds through the economy to benefit everyone else. Japan has to import more of its raw materials and energy than any other country and hence has to export to pay for the imports. So it seems likely that although the airport is going to benefit a minority directly it is a considerable minority and through them it benefits most other people. It is possible that a better site than Narita could have been chosen but with a population of one hundred million in a country about the size of the state of Montana with 80 per cent of its land mountainous it is unlikely that a site could have been chosen which would not inconvenience someone. So the airlines and the travellers and the government all had their own bubble-logic. So too did the displaced farmers. So too did the antigovernment protesters and those who cared for the environment. The result was a long-drawn-out battle that delayed the opening of the airport for years.

Figure 3

non-aligned polarities in tight frame

aligned polarities in loose frame

The rule of law

The most obvious way to ensure the alignment of interests is through the creation of laws that regulate behaviour. The idea is that the perceived law becomes part of the logic-bubble and hence the logically determined behaviour is consistent with this. In practice it is doubtful whether laws by themselves have much effect. They might be perceived as something to be obeyed or as something to be ignored (like many of the laws concerning motoring offences). Deterrents are created to build fear into the logic-bubble and for some people they do. But for many people they probably do not. The weakness of a deterrent is that the lawbreaker has to conceive of himself getting caught. And unfortunately that sort of foresight may never enter the immediate logic-bubble of a criminal. Laws work in a law-abiding community where obedience to the law is already part of the logic-bubble – but such obedience is not created by the law.

Taboo and superstition

Here the rules are internalised and supported by a fear that is irrational enough to resist conscious alteration. The Christian notion of guilt was a successful device to internalise laws and so ensure the desired behaviour. The problem with both taboo and guilt is that they are essentially negative. Like laws they tell people what they should *not* do and even when they prescribe positive actions these are usually trivial rituals. It is difficult to see how one could build the positive aspects of society on this sort of basis.

Leadership and authority

A leader may be a teacher who enlarges the perception of his followers so that they can look through their own individual logic-bubbles to glimpse a wider logic-bubble or so that they can include foresight in their own. A leader may exhort cooperation as the late President Jomo Kenyatta of Kenya did with his famous cry of 'Harrambee' (let's pull together). To provide such inspiration he needs a personal charisma. This builds the leader into the perception of his followers so that his wishes are obeyed just because they are his. Hero-worship and the mass hysteria engendered by sports or pop stars work in the same way to take over a significant part of the followers' logic-bubbles. It is difficult to imagine that this process could be achieved by respect for a sane and rational leader who governed with skill and wisdom. I suspect that leadership has always got to be mythical or larger than life because it is not affecting logic but the perceptions of the logic-bubble which then produce the logic.

Self-image

Self-image is probably one of the most effective methods for creating alignment of the polarity of logic-bubbles in society. Whether it is the image of the gentleman, the public-school boy, the officer, the Christian, the romantic, the Buddhist or the Zulu warrior the point is that a standard image is adopted as a self-image and hence the alignment of interests is automatic. It is no longer a matter of law, guilt, fear or leader inspiration. Moreover it is a positive factor that leads to constructive action rather, than just preventing negative action. It is of course the opposite of expediency and pragmatism and what-you-can-get-away-with. Probably the most powerful moments in the history of any society have occurred when this sort of self-image was consciously fostered, or arose. It is all tied in with honour and dignity but not necessarily with confidence or morale.

Group pressure

This is the other most effective method for aligning self-interest, at least with the interest of the group though not necessarily with that of society. To some extent the self-image method may partake of group pressure in the same way as a member of a club behaves in an appropriate fashion because he fears censure from his fellows or even expulsion. But this is certainly not the only basis for the success of the self-image method. From the point of view of society it should be said that group pressure does not necessarily work in favour of society. The gang of youths who casually attacked a Thai waiter in London as he walked home in the evening and kicked and stabbed him nearly to death were also subject to group pressure – pressure to perform and show they were as 'brave' as each other.

In a military situation the group pressure within the military group and outside it can be strong enough – as in the First World War – to send men singing to a very likely death at the front. But if there is a significant group against the war, or even a group of deserters, then the peer-group pressure works just as well in that direction.

The Japanese have never acquired the Western habit of the ego. Western egos are encouraged by religious systems that emphasise reward and punishment and an individual earning of salvation. The Japanese ego is the group ego: it exists only so far as it is aligned with the group. The logic-bubble is largely occupied by perception of one's group. The group may vary from moment to moment: family group, work group, travel group and so on. I am not sure whether the concept of the Samurai was seen as a group role or more as a self-image concept.

A sense of group identity is one type of group pressure. There is also the type that might arise in a small village or community. This is partly based on fear ('What will the neighbours say?') and partly on the filling of a standard role, which may or may not be sufficiently internalised to be a self-image ('You will have to go to the fete, dear, it is expected of you'). Communities need not be throbbing with a single dedication of purpose but the pressures for the alignment of interest are strong because of the close scrutiny. The ethic of what-you-can-get-away-with is not easy to operate in the fishbowl of a village.

Common purpose

Terrorist groups have an enemy, a mission and a common purpose. Their self-interest is aligned with the group interest. Their work and their life are so closely intertwined that each logic-bubble has, as it were, a common part relating to the mission. The Dunkirk spirit, the sense of pulling together and the backs-to-the-wall attitude are all appreciations of the aligning power of a common purpose. The reconstruction of both German and Japanese industry after the war probably benefited from the same alignment of interests. The logic-bubbles of both management and unions were aligned in their polarity. Small communes often succeed at first because there is the common purpose of survival but when this seems assured then individual logic-bubbles lose their alignment and actions are dictated by perceptions other than survival – for instance jealousies and leadership struggles.

The difficulty with a common purpose is that it cannot be imposed by persuasion or exhortation: it really has to arise from the situation. General purposes such as a 'better society' are much too vague to work. The purpose has to be immediate and concrete. It may be that the common purpose works because it allows people to work together in groups (since they all have the same goal) and then the group identity and group pressure effects take over to sustain the common purpose.

Discipline

A soldier in the army, an athlete in training or a monk in a monastery are subject to discipline that they have chosen for a purpose. Without the discipline the logic-bubble of the moment would tell the monk it was better to lie in bed at five in the morning than get up to say prayers. The logic-bubble of the soldier would tell him it was better to lie down in the field than to charge on the machine-gun post. The logic-bubble of the athlete might lead him to several pints of beer at the local pub. Once discipline has been established and internalised it acts as a sort of self-image. Action follows the bubble-logic of the discipline rather than that of natural inclinations. Nor is it a constant battle between natural inclinations and the discipline (though it may be for some people) for there is enjoyment in carrying through the logic of the discipline.

Discipline is often wrongly regarded as the carrying out of orders without question or the instilling of sufficient fear to bring about obedience. This is not discipline nor is the respect for authority. True discipline is almost an hypnotic process in which the will is taken over by another. It is instilled not by fear but by practice: that is to say practice in following an external will.

Self-discipline is the interaction of a self-image with a self that is as yet separate. In time the two may merge to give the 'gentleman' who does not have to cajole himself into behaving as such.

Routine

The habit of unthinking routine can carry us through actions that would not be dictated by the logic of the moment. The purpose of drill and training is to remove certain actions from the sphere of conscious decision. As such the routine actions have conditioning circumstances rather than a true logic-bubble. A logic-bubble involves perceptions and the action that logically follows from them. A conditioned action may follow from a set of antecedents but no choice is involved. With a logic-bubble it is assumed that a choice does exist but that the most appropriate or logical choice is usually made.

Religion

Over the ages religion has provided the most powerful meta-system to take people out of the self-interest of their own little systems in order to work for a higher goal. It has been extraordinarily effective, with martyrs going willingly to a cruel death because of their belief in this meta-system.

Religion includes many of the methods mentioned above. There is discipline and there is routine. In the Catholic Church there is leadership and also the charismatic leadership of the saints and the Virgin Mary. There is guilt and there is self-image. In the Protestant Church the emphasis is more on the self-image of the Protestant ethic; in the Buddhist Church it is on self-disipline and the conscious alteration of the logic-bubble. In smaller communities there is always peer group pressure. Then there is the common purpose which is re-inforced by persecution and religious conflicts.

Finally in religion there is perceptual change. In some religions we learn to see suffering as something to be enjoyed as a means of earning salvation. We may also learn to enlarge our logic-bubble to include not only the immediate surroundings but future heaven and a God who is watching us.

Many religions seek to create a disgust with self in order that the logic-bubble of the moment will be centred elsewhere. Other religions go further and seek the annihilation of self so that the ego falls back into the continuous rhythms of nature. These are all perceptual changes wrought through teaching, insight and training.

Incentives and channelled self-interest

The crudest method of aligning interests is that of implanting a reward somewhere in the logic-bubble so that the logical response will be to move in the direction of action dictated by that reward. In this way it is hoped to channel self-interest to a common goal alignment. Everyone is still acting in his own self-interest but in response to a doctored logic-bubble. The rewards could be called bribes or sweeteners.

Artificial incentives probably work well up to a point then the ratchet effect takes over and they get taken for granted. Some people resent the stakhanovite pressure of working towards a reward. The main problem with incentives is that they are forever competing in the logic-bubble with other perceptions and at any moment peer-group pressure or a football match may dominate the logic-bubble. Incentives may work well at transition points but they do not work well on a sustained basis.

Negative incentives or threats against groups are virtually useless because they provide a common cause and strengthen peer-group pressures which will usually be stronger.

Perceptual change

Since a logic-bubble is the total sum of perceptions at that moment we could seek to change the polarity by changing the perceptions. You are hungry and you see a piece of chicken on the sideboard. Taking everything else into account, your logic-bubble dictates that you eat it. But if someone happens to mention that it is probably contaminated with salmonella your perceptions are changed and so is the action. As soon as you see a paper tiger to be a paper tiger your action is going to be different. The purpose of salesmanship or persuasion is, of course, to bring about such perceptual change. If you see things differently you act differently.

There are two ways of bringing about perceptual change. We can either increase the breadth and depth or we can change what we see. In the first case we may want to increase the breadth so we look at things from a less egocentric point of view or we may increase the depth so we can look further ahead and see the consequences of our actions. The CoRT (Cognitive Research Trust) thinking lessons used in schools act in this way. They are designed to act on perception. For example one boy in a Borstal institute changed his mind about absconding after applying one of the thinking lessons: his logic-bubble had been changed by his own ability to look at things more broadly.

The second way to alter perceptions is to be able to change the way we look at a particular thing: the glass is half-full rather than half-empty; the fact that a particular appliance is always breaking down is an opportunity to design a better one; a car is not a transport device but a status symbol. This changing of perceptions is what lateral thinking is all about.

Changing perceptions may also include changing values. Being loud and coarse may change from being a sign of machismo to being a sign of being loud and coarse. Getting away with a fraud may not be clever but anti-social. Making money may become achievement rather than exploitation. Dropping out may become a sign of feebleness. Ostentation may become vigour rather than vulgarity. The sneer may become laughable rather than smart. The negative mind may become mediocre rather than clever.

System design and logic-bubbles

The aim of social system design is both to make use of the natural polarity of logic-bubbles and to encourage the development of a positive polarity. For example if the idiom in education is that of conformity and the right-answer-game, then anyone who is not good at this automatically becomes cast as a rebel. He sees himself in the role of rebel, truant and outsider and this sets up and determines his logic-bubbles thereafter. In industry the organisation of work on a group basis as tried by Volvo in Sweden creates a different logic-bubble that now includes peer pressure acting in a positive way, whereas before it might have tended to act in a negative way (workers against management). It should be noted that system design of this sort is quite different from the writing of further laws and their stricter enforcement. It may be thought to come under the heading of manipulation; but is the building of a new road manipulation because it allows cars to travel in a preferable direction?

The design or emphasis of roles is part of this design process. The creation of an appropriate role allows the occupier to develop a self-image in that role (if the design is strong enough) and a sense of responsibility, and both of these play a determining part in his logic-bubbles. For example there are few urban equivalents of the country doctor or the parish priest. The nearest – and for a very limited sector of society – is the American analyst who is a paid listener. Perhaps we could have more paid listeners who would not presume to be advisers. The effectiveness of the Samaritan movement is something along these lines: skilled listening with some commonsense advice.

Philosophy and world-view

There are conscious philosophies such as existentialism and less conscious ones such as regarding the state as a sort of super-parent who has the duty to provide but must expect no contribution. The world-view reflects the mood of the age, the family background and the peer culture. It does not alter or override the logic-bubble as such but it does develop the perceptions and values that go to make up the 'wall' of the logic bubble. To change a logic-bubble it may be much more effective to work at this level than to try to alter an established bubble by feeding in incentives or fear.

With the lessening of influence of the major religions the world-view has no definite focus of development. There are a number of enthusiastic sects, some politico-religious groups, occasional outbursts of 'improve-me' secular religions in the USA (like 'est') and a general day-to-day mild hedonism which regards the future as too complex to do much about. In the background are some powerful ideals concerned with care for the environment and care for others. It is difficult to be sure how widespread these are. Certainly they are significant enough to be mobilised as in anti-nuclear-power-station demonstrations. Pop culture is real enough and probably corresponds most closely to religious enthusiasm. It is felt rather than conceptualised.

Boredom, lack of purpose and confusion have replaced material suffering – in the developed countries – as the seed-ground for a new philosophy. But boredom can be alleviated by day-to-day distractions, kicks and gimmicks, whereas suffering required a more sustained world-view philosophy. There is no lack of credulity for there is a growing interest in the bizarre, the extra-terrestrial and such matters as astrology. There is a yearning for a semi-scientific religion that cannot be dominated by the experiments and pronouncements of scientists.

Emotion, feeling and logic-bubbles

The interplay of emotion and perception is a complicated one. Initial perception triggers emotion which then controls the development of further perception. For example you see a man in your house. You recognise he is not a friend and at once the emotion of fear takes over. Fear now fills out the rest of your perceptions with images and suppositions and remembered pieces of newspaper stories. I think it is easiest to regard emotion as part of perception: it is just non-conceptualised perception. A name of a holiday resort may elicit images of what you have experienced at that resort but it may equally elicit a general feeling of pleasure and enjoyment.

Emotions are alterable through perceptual alteration and change of circumstance. Peoples who fought one another in a war are happy to do business with each other. The first day at school is full of terrors but as you learn how things work these evaporate.

Emotions are part of the total set of perceptions that constitute the logic-bubbles. Would anyone ever do anything which was inconsistent with his emotions of the moment? The answer is obviously yes. A terrified soldier may yet be brave in battle. A frightened secretary may yet answer her boss's call on the intercom. An angry host may yet be polite to his guests. A hating child may yet obey his parent. Emotions are part of the total logic-bubble and may be over-ridden if the other perceptions are dominant.

Confusion, which is an emotion usually not described as such, arises when there are competing logic-bubbles which cannot yet be integrated into a single one. Conflicting perceptions, conflicting roles and conflicting emotions may serve to set up alternative sets of perceptions. Indecision is itself the logical outcome of a particular set of circumstances – even though it is not much use as a basis for action.

Roles, compartments and logic-bubbles

A person playing different roles may switch from one logic-bubble to another. A logic-bubble is the assembled perceptions at that moment, not a sort of carapace of soul which a person forever carries around with him. Westerners tend to integrate their experience and moods into a single soul which may be carried to all situations. The Japanese who do not seem to have this ego development find it easier to enjoy a different 'soul' for each type of situation or role. The souls are like alternative books on a library shelf. At home the Japanese man is a traditional family man, probably subservient to his wife in many matters (for example she takes all the pay packet and doles him out what he needs weekly for bus fares and cigarettes); at the office he may be a Western style business man; out and about in the evening he may be a hedonist. In this way he can surrender himself fully to each situation instead of standing outside it with his 'averaging' soul.

The type of logic-bubble used in one role may be quite different from that used in another. A corrupt lawyer may yet be a good lawyer when he is not playing the greedy role. A law-abiding citizen who switches into the role of a criminal may use logic-bubbles appropriate to that role once he has made the switch. The deterrents are designed to deter him from making that switch. Once he has made the switch his logic-bubble now tells him that he is clever enough not to get caught.

At first it must seem that compartmentalisation must lead to chaos on a Jekyll-and-Hyde level. Any behaviour can be excused on the ground that it was the responsibility of a different self. The whole purpose of the integrated Christian soul with its guilt was to avoid this. On the positive side it might be possible to create positive roles that can be played as such even though there is no total conversion of the person playing that role.

Summary

In this chapter I have sought to outline the 'notation' concept of the logic-bubble. The purpose of doing this is to suggest that a person is indeed acting sensibly and intelligently within his own logic-bubble of the moment. Therefore accusations of stupidity, condemnation and hope for change are all largely irrelevant: they are all akin to saying, 'Please act unintelligently within your perceptions of the moment.' At first sight this must seem a passive and fatalistic view which excuses anyone his or her actions on the basis that such actions are perfectly logical behaviour under the circumstances. In fact the approach clarifies matters and helps us to decide how best to develop beneficial perceptions and how to alter logic-bubbles to avoid the clashes of self-interest in society. Nor does it mean that an action has to be accepted at any moment because it is too late to alter the logic-bubble. The logic-bubble consists of the perceptions at the moment and into these can be fed an objection to the contemplated action. Punishment is valid not as revenge but as architecture for future logic-bubbles.

I do not believe that multiplication of laws as such is particularly effective. I do not think that incentives are very useful except at transition points. It is unlikely that a common purpose of the 'Dunkirk' type can be drummed up. Nor do I feel that the strong meta-system of religion can be revived through evangelism. On the other hand I do feel that no society is strong enough to allow for the jungle clash of conflicting self-interest.

The most hopeful area would be peer-group pressure although this has the danger that it can so easily work either way (boy-scouts or bikies). System design is of the utmost importance as also is role design. We may succeed in developing a sense of purpose but it will probably be at local level rather than national level. The development of a strong and positive self-image would be ideal because of its power. It is a difficult – but perhaps not impossible – task.

A change in world-view and philosophy may happen but left to the natural flow of events there is no way of telling whether this will be in a positive direction or otherwise. This would seem to be an area where art, literature and the media could have a responsibility (this matter will be considered later). Perceptual change is a hopeful approach and we can certainly do something about that in education though at the moment we are doing very little. When we talk about moral tone we are really talking about the alignment of polarity of logic-bubbles in the sense that immediate self-interest includes moral considerations. It may be that in the future the moral tone will be concerned with developing a world that is fit to live in rather than a soul that is fit to get to heaven. Yet somehow self-interest has to be brought into it. After all, getting to heaven is very much a matter of self-interest. That is why the self-image concept described in my book *The Happiness Purpose* could be important.

We need to be concerned at a much earlier stage than the altering of already established logic-bubbles by law, punishment or incentive. It is at the ingredient stage that the greatest effect can be made. What are the perceptions that will be used moment to moment in the future to form the logic-bubbles? In addition to the attention to perception we may want to provide the sort of 'over-ride' whereby a logic-bubble indicating one course of action can be overridden by a combination of self-image and discipline (usually called 'will').

Do we seek to alter car design, or build new roads, or just increase the traffic regulations?

6 THE EDGE EFFECT

The edge effect is something to do with the journey of one thousand miles that still has to start with a single pace.

A clockwork toy car does not fall off the table – it falls off the edge of the table. The edge to action is what you do first and when you have done that the edge is what you do next and after that what you do next. When you come to a roundabout you have to choose the road off it. There is an 'edge' decision. Once you have chosen the road then you proceed along it.

We are pretty good at thinking of destinations and goals and ultimate objectives – even utopias. But we are not so good at planning the very first step that may need to be taken. One aspect of the genius of Karl Marx was that he put more emphasis and enjoyment on the struggle against capitalism than on the paradise that was going to come about once capitalism had collapsed.

Imagine that Paradise City has been pointed out to you. It lies fifty miles down a clear road. You set off down the road but after a few yards you come to a ditch that is deep and about ten yards wide. Now ten yards is not much to set against a journey of fifty miles: it is only a tiny fraction of the way. Nevertheless you cannot cross the ditch. So although you are convinced that you are on the right road and that Paradise City is well worth reaching you cannot proceed because you cannot cross the 'edge'. Making Paradise City more attractive or improving the road beyond the ditch is of no value.

A woman has a terrible time with her husband who beats and ill-treats her. She has friends she can go and stay with. But she cannot leave her husband without telling him and she cannot face the moment of telling him. So the intolerable situation continues because of the edge effect.

Great plans are made for a new airport and many experts are consulted. But when the site is finally chosen for the third London airport the residents of a small village mount a protest campaign which is taken up in the media and the site is abandoned. Although the idea is economically sound it has proved impossible to cross the edge.

Imagine again that road to Paradise City but this time there is no ditch. Instead after you have gone a few yards there is a terrible stench. The stench is not a physical barrier like the ditch. You can continue walking along the road if you want to. But you do not want to. The stench puts you off. The attractions of the distant Paradise City fade before the immediacy of the stench. Of course you have no way of telling that the stench only lasts for fifty yards and that you can almost hold your breath for that distance. So with a scheme there may be an almost physical barrier at the edge or there may be an edge that is simply unpleasant or temporarily disadvantageous.

So in much of our planning the transition state or edge is even more important than the final destination, for unless the edge can be crossed the attraction of the utopia becomes irrelevant. It also follows that any path of change that involves an initial difficult or unattractive edge will probably not be followed. That places a terrible restriction on evolution because many forms of change involve at least some temporary disadvantage for an established interest. The same thing was mentioned right at the beginning of the book with regard to the story of the land-rover which was not allowed to drive South.

In a democracy with sensitive media the effect is enhanced. Any form of censorship whatever – for example a suggestion that

TV should ban violence – is met with a howl of outrage on the basis that once a principle is breached then it is probably lost.

In Northern Ireland, in Rhodesia and in South Africa there are stalemates because of the edge effect. Any suggested change must seem to be a disadvantage for those in control. Nor is there any way of knowing whether this disadvantage would merely be a transition stage or whether it would escalate to disaster.

Many people are shy or timid about joining groups. They cannot cross this edge so they never join. Yet if they do join they will find that the timidity disappears. In any case if they do not like the group they can always leave.

So the first type of edge effect concerns a desired action which cannot be undertaken because there exists an edge which cannot be crossed.

As a final example let us take the instance of lung cancer and cigarette smoking. Most medical authorities seem convinced that cigarette smoking is largely responsible for deaths from lung cancer and probably a contributory factor in deaths from cardiovascular diseases and some respiratory diseases. In 1976 there were 38,000 lung cancer deaths in the UK. This compared with 7,600 deaths from road accidents. If there were to be a change in car design which resulted in a fourfold increase in road accident fatalities the change would be banned immediately. Yet we could not ban cigarettes even if we were convinced that the lung cancer deaths are mainly caused by smoking. There is an edge that is difficult to cross. Many people enjoy smoking and many smoke in amounts so small that they would not consider themselves at risk. The tobacco industry could not be dismantled overnight. The government would miss the large tax bite that comes from tobacco. Even banning smoking in all public places – as is done in some countries – is not possible because it would be unpopular with so many people. The compulsory use of seat belts in cars has not been instituted – as it has in countries like Australia – because there would be an initial outcry about restricted freedom.

In some cases we can see that there is an edge but we cannot cross it. In others we are not sure whether it is just an edge or whether it may turn out to be the wrong road.

The edge effect and continuity

A pharmaceutical company comes up with a new treatment for a particular disease. No one is sure whether the treatment is of much use because it has not yet been tried in man and animals never get this particular disease. A controlled trial is set up in which half the patients are to get the new treatment and the other half are to go without. In proper scientific fashion the doctor running the trial does not know which patients are getting the treatment and which are not because the patients are assigned at random to each group and then one group is given the injections and the other group is given dummy injections which look exactly the same. All is ready for the important trial. Then one day the doctor is faced with a patient who is severely ill with the disease. He is at the 'edge of action'. He knows that the patient may die, from his past experience of the disease. He knows that the new treatment has not been shown to be effective. But there is just a chance that it might make a difference. He feels he cannot deny the patient the chance, so he breaks the code and makes sure that the injections used are the effective ones, not the dummy ones. Having done this on one occasion he knows that he will never be able to deny a patient this treatment in order to carry through the proper trial. It also becomes very difficult for anyone else to deny the treatment to a seriously ill patient so the required trial is never carried out. With the new treatment the mortality rate is not radically changed but there may just be a difference. Comparison of pre-treatment results with the results of the new treatment is not sufficient to prove the effectiveness of the treatment. Although it is a very expensive treatment it goes on being used because it just might be effective and no proper trial can now be done.

New machines are installed to print a newspaper. The machines require far fewer men to work them so the men go on strike fearing loss of their specialised jobs. The machinery is idle and the paper loses money every day. It also loses circulation and advertising to competing papers. The demands of the moment or the 'edge' make the management give in and so there is an agreement that more men than are actually required will work the presses. Some years later the productivity introduced by the new machines can no longer give enough profit margin for the employment of excess workers. But any attempt to reduce manning leads to an immediate threat of strike. Something set up because of one edge effect must continue because of another edge effect. A major newspaper in New York went out of business precisely because of this effect. What is interesting is that both management and workers were locked into the situation.

So the edge effect may mean that something must continue because no one may dare to discontinue it at any particular moment though in general that is desired. This is another instance of the Catch-23 mentioned earlier: it is essential that something gets done but it never makes sense to do it at any particular moment.

Continuity also means that something gets done at a particular moment (edge) because not doing it would cause problems. So an individual in a gang of teenagers dare not hang back when they are kicking to death an innocent passer-by because hanging back would threaten his position in the gang.

The edge effect may insist that something has to be done at that moment. In 1975 the health service in the UK spent £3.5 million on appetite suppressant pills, while the government spent £1.2 million in total on education research. The appetite suppressant pills are not very effective in the long run but there is an edge effect when the doctor in his surgery is faced by an overweight and depressed patient who claims to have dieted to no effect and who pleads with him to give her something to reduce her appetite.

In the United States there is a burst of ecological pressure so some action has to be taken. There is an edge. The simplest governmental action – which offends no one – is to ask for a report or to set up a department. So there is now an Environmental Protection Agency, a Council of Environmental Quality, and a Temporary Commission on Air Quality. Once set up, such structures tend to continue, since discontinuing them arouses protest because the government will seem to be weakening on the issue.

The edge effect and accretion

At a roundabout you have to decide which road to take off it. That is one sort of edge effect. But once you have taken a road then you tend to move along that road with continuity. Once you have started to dig a hole in a place you tend to enlarge that same hole bit by bit. You are unlikely to abandon the hole to start digging somewhere entirely new. This is an analogy I used in one of my first books. This commitment to a direction is perfectly reasonable. It is partly a matter of investment in that direction. It is partly that the road ahead seems very clear. It is partly that what you do generates further work to be done. In a sense the 'edge' is now the rim of the hole or the edge of the road and it is difficult to cross it.

Someone produces a philosophical thesis. Then there is a refutation followed by a counter-refutation. Then restatement of the thesis in a more exact form. Then commentary upon commentary and review. Then the implications of the theory and in turn each implication generates its own activity. So the series proceeds getting ever more refined and ever more remote (like following a road through all its windings into the remote hinterland because that is where the road takes you. You cannot easily step off because the excitement and action carry you forward. To step out of the idiom is to be out of the game). The journals and the book reviewers come to expect material that continues the thrust and all else is rejected. The apostolic succession ensures that the new professor of philosophy is fit and proper to play the current game. And so the continuity carries forward.

The same thing happens in research. Someone focuses on a new chemical. Its presence is measured in all possible situations and disease states. Its effect on metabolism is studied. Controlled trials are done to assess its effect. There are confirmatory experiments and negative experiments. The relationship of this chemical to other chemicals is studied. All of it is inevitable. Knowledge spawns knowledge in a geometric progression. Research departments and PhD students are anxious to have a 'tight' project they can work upon. It is not difficult to convince yourself that what you are working on could have the greatest importance. Others more distant from the battle-front know that useful knowledge might turn up from something that seems a bit peripheral at the moment and if they forget it they will be given numerous examples of unexpected break-throughs and valuable spin-offs. So research continues edging forward bit by bit from where it is at the moment. The fact that there are areas of major importance which are more or less neglected does not matter. There is nothing happening in those areas – there is no edge from which to move forward.

An artist appears. The critics take a look at his work. If it is not new it is not worthy of attention. So they pick out something new, especially if it opens up a whole new area of theorising and writing because that is the work-area of the critics (as described so well by Tom Wolfe in his article 'The Painted Word'). So to get attention there must be something that is different from what has gone before. So art moves ahead with each artist trying to establish his difference in order to get attention. So art, like philosophy and science, becomes ever more peripheral. There are no villains. It is the nature of the system. Art would be different if there were no art critics. Philosophy would be different if philosophers did not have to publish in journals and aspire to be selected by their peers for chairs of philosophy. Science would be different if research subjects were allocated on the basis of the importance of the area.

The creeping effect of moment to moment continuity is shown in any situation where something happens gradually without there ever being a sharp point of decision or protest. The effect of inflation on fiscal drag has been mentioned before. As incomes rise with inflation the low incomes rise into higher tax bands so we find the equivalent of the government raising taxes sharply even for average earners. But the process is perceived gradually and there is no sharp point of decision or protest. The government has done nothing wrong – merely failed to correct a naturally occurring injustice which is to its benefit. In 1970/71 in the UK the tax yield was £5,731 million and in 1976/77 it was £17,013 million – a rise which was well ahead of inflation. In 1976 four times as many people were paying higher rates of tax as in 1972.

The edge effect and individuals

It is claimed that the famous Oldham test-tube baby (fertilisation of the ovum by a sperm outside the body) cost the taxpayers £64,000. With a health service very short of money this could be regarded as a peripheral luxury. After all there are enough babies being born in the usual way to make such heroic measures unnecessary. Yet if you were the desperate mother concerned, if you were at the 'edge' of the situation, you might think differently.

It has been shown that the level of unemployment has no effect on the wage equation in spite of what economists predict about unemployment holding down wages. Those in jobs do not conceive of unemployment. The unemployed do that. So also in a survey the main concern was inflation not unemployment.

In general the building industry might be in favour of innovation. But on any particular building the contractor and the owner are against innovation if it is going to cost money or increase the building time. They ask why they should bear the cost of innovation from which subsequent builders are going to benefit.

This whole aspect might be considered as a rider on Catch-23: it is desirable that something should (or should not) be done – so long as it does not affect me personally. Increasing the traffic through an airport may be essential so long as you do not live on the edge of the airport. The citizens at home encourage the war but it is the soldiers at the edge of action who get killed. Conversely, the car at the edge of the junction considerately allows the other cars to roll by, but the cars at the end of the long queue behind him fume at the delay. Travellers at the front end of a queue for a train do not object too strongly to the occasional what-you-can-get-away-with artist who drifts his way into the queue because they know it will not much affect their chance of getting on to the train. But the people at the far end of the queue know that every queue jumper can significantly alter their chances.

The edge effect and practical action

Everyone can theorise and agree that it would be a good thing if schools were to pay more attention to thinking skills – but what matters is at the edge of action. What happens on Monday morning at 8.30 am when you are facing a class of thirty pupils? That is the edge of action and you have to have a concrete step-by-step method, not an agreed theory.

Similarly the salesman who is setting out to visit a school to sell materials for his publisher might be enthusiastic about the teaching of thinking but at the practical edge of action who does he ask to see at the school? There is a Geography teacher and a Mathematics teacher but no one with the responsibility for teaching thinking.

What does the doctor do at the practical edge of action when he knows that what the patient needs is a pill that has no effect at all but acts as a placebo? Useful as it might be, no such pill could ever exist because it would be denounced as a fraud, so he prescribes unnecessary vitamins, at a cost, because they will do no harm.

At the practical edge of action the doctor in the United States orders X-rays and every other conceivable test after an injury not because he feels them necessary – nor indeed just to earn money – but because if he did not and the patient were to sue him the damages would be enormous. So the huge wastage goes on.

The shop steward is not dealing with job satisfaction in the abstract but with working conditions and working people at the practical edge of action.

In many countries the temptation of bribery is at the practical edge of action. If you don't accept the money someone else will, and anyway everyone else is doing it.

This aspect of the edge effect also works the other way. If you are involved in a smooth running routine that requires minimum exertion and in which the problems have long since been ironed out, why should you drop that in favour of an unproved innovation which is likely to involve effort, hassle and risk just because someone tries to convince you that – in the long run – it will benefit the organisation or society? The edge effect is concerned with 'now' and not with the long run.

The edge-effect effect and logic-bubbles

There is obviously an overlap between the edge effect and logic-bubbles. The edge effect is more general and refers to systems as well as to people. It is concerned with continuity as well as barriers to change. A logic-bubble is concerned with the perceptions that logically determine action at any moment. Such perceptions will obviously include perceptions of the edge involved (like the ditch across the road to Paradise City or the bad stench). It is because we operate through logic-bubbles that the edge effect is so strong.

Summary

In this chapter I have sought to point out the reality of what I have called the 'edge effect'. There is nothing novel, surprising or complicated about it. But we pay far too little attention to it. We regard it as the necessary cement between the bricks of our social architecture but I believe it to be as important as, and in practice more important than, the bricks. Unless we pay deliberate attention to it, all else is theoretical. Consider that no matter how large a mass of ice may be and in whatever climate, it will be kept from melting so long as its edge is kept perfectly insulated. Conversely, once it starts melting at the edge then eventually it will all melt away.

To devise mechanisms for dealing positively with the edge effect is not difficult. Zero-base budgeting, discretionary budgets of time and money, transition subsidies, priority reviews, planning from the edge outwards and many other methods spring to mind once we are decided to do something about it. Lack of attention to the area makes change impossible and it also results in a great deal of wasted effort especially in peripheralism.

It also follows that once change starts moving in the right direction then like a 'positive' epidemic it can spread. Pop culture worked like that.

7 PROVOCATION AND PO

'Po' is a created word that I have used, and described, in several of my books. It is derived from words like possible, hypothesis, suppose, poetry and positive. In all of these situations we use ideas or images in order to move forward, in order to see what we can produce, in order to see where they get us. In no case is the use of the idea put forward as an accurate description of what things are.

The process is one of provocation. We put forward an idea as a provocation to get us out of a fixed set of ideas so that we can think of new ones. From a mathematical point of view provocation is essential in a patterning system. Indeed provocation is part of the logic of such a system. I have attempted to explain this aspect in my book *The Mechanism of Mind*. Many people understand the attitude of lateral thinking but not the process. Imagine you are on a misty hill-top and when the mist clears you notice someone standing there with you. He tells you he arrived by helicopter. If you do not know about helicopters you will rightly condemn him for using a 'fancy' word to describe climbing up the hill-side as you yourself have done and countless other people like you. Similarly, lateral thinking is concerned with looking at things in a different way, with alternatives and with new ideas. But that is only the end-point. The actual processes arise directly from consideration of the behaviour of a self-organising pattern-making system like the mind. And all the evidence is that it is a pattern-making system – otherwise (like computers) we should be unable to laugh.

Provocation is closely related to humour for humour suddenly reveals to us how we can see something in a different way: like a child's riddle or a pun at the lower level and sophisticated wit at the higher level.

Provocation is a sort of mental experiment. We decide to look at something in a novel way in order to see where it gets us. There may not be a reason for saying something until after it has been said. In other words the statement is not the cumulative conclusion of a series of rational steps. It is a provocation and if it leads to something useful then that is the justification for the statement in the first place. In this instance the end does justify the means.

We need a language indicator to show that we are behaving in this irresponsible manner. The word 'po' is, I accept, no more felicitous than any other sharp syllable might be. But it is a definite enough indicator. By sheer chance the syllable 'po' does have a symbol in Linear B, the ancient Minoan language. This symbol is related to the sound for horse and shows a horse's head of a sort. Perhaps in time we might introduce this symbol as a new punctuation mark at the beginning of a sentence to indicate that the sentence is meant to be a provocation. It would be like a reverse question mark. Figure 4 shows the symbol. I have always found a deal of logic in the Spanish habit of putting a question mark at the beginning, as well as at the end, of a sentence. If we were to use such a symbol then the word 'po' would be unnecessary in writing.

Let us look at some very simple provocations. They will be made deliberately extreme in order to illustrate the process. In practice a provocation may be extreme or it may be more or less reasonable. We watch an aeroplane landing and we might say: 'po planes should land upside down'.There is no reason for saying this except that it is a facile distortion of the usual state of affairs. But we work from the provocation and see what ideas follow. Normally a plane lands by reducing speed and so reducing lift on the wings. It thus sinks onto the ground. The idea of 'landing upside down' might suggest that the plane as it were 'rose' onto the ground just as, normally, it rose into the air. So there might be some positive downward lift which would be finely controlled to give delicate landings. I do not know if there is any positive value in this idea or whether the difficulties would, in practice, outweigh any advantages. If I was involved in aircraft design I might do some simple experiments and considerations to look into it.

Figure 4

po symbol

po cars should have square wheels

cars should have square wheels

Motor car wheels are round for obvious reasons. As a provocation we might say: 'po wheels should be square'. This is patently absurd and we could dismiss it outright. Or we could play the game and just see if it led to any interesting notion. Square wheels would be impossible for rolling but they offer a much larger area in contact with the ground and this could be helpful in wet weather, in braking or whenever improved adhesion was required. Could we, somehow, keep this advantage and yet make the wheel usable as a wheel? We could: by having an inner tyre which was inflated to the usual pressure and which supported the axle in the usual way. But, as a rim outside this tyre would be another tyre, which was inflated to a much lower pressure (or even fluid-filled). This outer tyre would act like a partially deflated tyre with a much larger area in contact with the ground. Again the idea may not be worth the bother. It might offer no advantages over a partially deflated tyre. But the idea now exists and it can be thought about. It might lead to an even better idea.

For the control of inflation we might say: 'Po, it would be nice to have a sort of "timid" money which withdrew from the market place at the first sign of inflation'. This leads on to ideas some of which will be described later.

I have introduced the concept of provocation at this stage in the book in order to explain some of the ideas that follow. Some of them are meant quite seriously, some are meant semi-seriously and some are intended as outright provocations. In all cases my hope is that the ideas may lead to other – and possibly better – ideas in the mind of the reader. I am aware that this may be regarded as a clever dodge to defuse criticism – and of course it is.

Since I do not intend to indicate which ideas I am offering seriously and which are meant as provocations (I shall usually omit 'po') the negative mind will risk wasting its well-aimed fusillade on what was only meant as a provocation – and hence show its inability to understand the game. The positive mind, on the other hand, will have no such difficulty. The positive mind will accept ideas which seem worthwhile as useful starting points for consideration. The ideas that do not seem worthwhile will be treated as provocations to be used to generate other ideas that may be interesting if not wonderful. I hope I have never seemed to claim a monopoly on the ability to generate new ideas.

As I mentioned in a previous chapter, I believe the CYA attitude (only say things bland enough or sufficiently on the side of the angels to be protected against a kick in the pants) is a dangerous reaction to rampant negativity. 'Po' is a counter-attack and puts the onus on the intelligent mind to use its vaunted skill in a positive and constructive manner.

8 CONCEPTS AND BATTLE-CRIES

Any civilisation maintains a stock of basic concepts. These provide the basic principles to guide choice and development and they also provide the battle-cries. The concepts are generally abstract and most people do not give them a moment's thought provided they feel someone else is looking after them. From time to time the concepts are flaunted as battle-cries to block one suggested change or to urge another. Concepts like 'freedom' provide splendid battle-cries.

A concept is like a major city. It arises from a need and at a convenient spot. Once established it grows through success and trade. It monopolises all the traffic around and all activity must pass through it. You cannot avoid the city for the roads lead that way. No other town can exist nearby because the major city dominates it and bleeds away its business. Occasionally we might try and create a by-pass which will allow us to detour around a town that has become confusing to traverse. So it is with concepts that dominate the traffic of ideas. To tamper with them is, of course, sacrilege.

Like banners most concepts are usable if they are held at arm's length up in the air so that everyone else can see them.

It must be admitted that concepts like 'freedom' make splendid banners or battle-cries because they do not need defining, they can be used for most situations and no one can be against them. We can conceive, however, that there might be a difference between a battle-cry and an operating principle. It is quite possible to have swords that are less than optimal ploughshares or generals who make poor politicians.

We can certainly shape social progress by the judicious shouting of the right battle-cry at the right moment but the whole concept of shaping by opposition and protest may need examining. Consider a skilled craftsman who gets on with the job once the broad outlines of the requirements have been given to him. The less we interfere with him the better. Consider next a moderately good craftsman and here advice and correction will probably improve his performance. Consider last an incompetent craftsman and here any amount of interference and pressure will not produce a good result. When we seek to mould society by protest and pressure we suppose that it has a great deal of energy and skilled craftsmen who are guiding its destiny. For time to time we may be right in that supposition – but we may also be wrong. Battle-cries by themselves are not constructive and do not positively design a better society.

As a start we might take the three concepts that together provided the battle-cry of the French Revolution.

Freedom

Freedom is the invaluable battle-cry that underpins all thought of social development and spearheads all revolution. Like water it is intensely desirable in thirst but taken for granted otherwise. As a battle-cry against tyranny it is focused and sharp and needs no elaboration. As an operating principle it is vague and ill-defined.

It may be that there is no such thing as freedom – it is merely a marketing expression for no-tyranny. It may be that we do not actually want to eat anchovies but we cannot tolerate anyone forbidding us to eat anchovies or forcing us to eat them.

It may be that today we should be growing aware of new tyrannies: the tyrannies of complexity, of interference and of endless form-filling. It may be that complexity can provide an overdose of apparent freedom. There may be people who do not wish to be bullied by opportunities, forced to make decisions and allowed to make mistakes.

Should a person be free to commit suicide and free to take heroin? In British Columbia there are said to be between 7,000 and 10,000 drug addicts. There is a suggested programme of three years' forced treatment with up to six months' detention if necessary. The cost would be £7 million. Perhaps we implicitly accept the notion that man should be free to be positive but not free to be negative. It is certainly a workable idiom. In the end it comes down to a matter of perception and of definition. Is heroin-addiction a disease as surely as small-pox is a disease or is it a freely chosen activity? The onus should perhaps be on the defenders of heroin use, to defend it in terms of its positive value and not in terms of freedom.

Is there much difference between the deaths from heroin and the many thousands that die each year from lung cancer through exercising their right to smoke cigarettes in spite of the health warnings? The answer is a cynical one. Lung cancer is perceived as a disease of relatively old age and one is going to die anyway. If 38,000 people under the age of forty died each year from lung cancer in the UK the response might be different.

We accept a large number of injuries from road accidents because that is a price that has to be paid for the benefits of mobility. Yet if the motor-cycle accident rate is about thirty times as great as that for cars is that an acceptable cost? The figure is probably not nearly as high if parallel age groups are considered but a significant difference must remain. Should people be free to fasten their seat belts or not, or to smoke freely in public places? Many of these apparent restrictions of freedom can be supported on the basis of the cost to society and any cost to society is automatically a cost to everyone else.

Many London squares have become dogs' lavatories. Dog owners in London have nowhere else to exercise their dogs and so the result is inevitable. Some of these squares have, as a result, become unfit for children to use. There is an asymmetry: children do not render such places unusable by dogs but dogs render them unusable by children. In New York the authorities decided that dog owners should be personally responsible for picking up the dog excreta which their pets left on the sidewalks or in the parks. Very soon the number of dogs turned in to animal shelters increased by thirty per cent. Many dog owners were not prepared to pay the price of freedom to own a dog.

Parents whose children are fond of ponies soon get subjected to the 'tyranny' of the horse routine: grooming, exercising, shows and the lot. Most other hobbies or sports have their own tyrannies or their own price to pay. To be free to choose a particular tyranny is freely to be subjected to it no matter how tyrannical it is in objective terms. A monk may be subject to a rigorous discipline but he has freedom because he has chosen the discipline. The same applies to a soldier who volunteers to join the army. All of them, as it were, pay a price for their choice. In short freedom is not free.

There is a great deal of wisdom in Henry Ford's famous remark (quoted earlier in the book) that consumers could choose any colour they wanted – so long as it was black. To choose freely what is readily available must be a major ingredient in both freedom and happiness. The concept would arouse an outcry on the basis that it could soon lead to: 'This is what you are offered, take it or leave it.' It may have been the price of the paint but it is rather more likely that Ford chose black because most people had already shown that they preferred black – so he was following their free choice not forcing it.

In any case those who were not willing to accept the benefits of Ford's cheap cars could, no doubt, buy another colour from another maker at a rather higher price. So once again their freedom of choice would have a price – as indeed it does in any commercial sense.

In Italy in 1978 there were 46,000 architecture students for an estimated 2,500 jobs in architecture. The students had exercised their free choice in choosing a subject and they were (one hopes) aware of the job situation.

In some other countries there is an allocation of university places according to the need for physicists, doctors, engineers and so on. In such cases the students earn the right to choose a particular subject by hard work and academic attainment (which may be a poor sort of selection since an academic doctor is not necessarily a good one). But if a state can afford the luxury of free choice in this matter then that is part of the quality of life that is the purpose of a state. Much depends on the notion of the priorities of resource allocation.

A doctor earns his right to practise as a doctor by years of training and competence-testing in examinations. The ordinary concept of compulsory education is to compel parents to give their children the right to be educated. But looked at another way, education could be the means by which a youngster earned his freedom to be a competent citizen. We should then have to re-organise, rather radically, the content of education.

The concept of earned freedom will also be explored in a later part of the book.

In general, society has not been very good at developing the concept of alternative life-styles and the option to choose freely the style that suits one's needs. It follows, as with a monk or a soldier, that once the choice is made the requirements of that particular life-style will be freely observed. In other words freedom is concentrated at the point of choice. The complexity would be enormous if society contained alternative parallel life-styles with different tax systems and everything else. But that is just the sort of complexity that computerisation makes possible.

If freedom is an absence of tyranny then with the concept of 'rights' we move into a more formal contractual arrangement. Rights are synonymous with expectations, and expectations imply that there is an obligation or duty for someone to fulfil that contract. There is a difference between the freedom to go to hell and the right to demand a vehicle to get you there. The United States Declaration of Independence, which is very concerned with rights (life, liberty and the pursuit of happiness), does not make clear whether citizens are to be free to enjoy these rights or whether they have the right to demand that the state provides the wherewithal. There is a crucial difference between the right to keep your earnings and the right to have earnings provided for you. It is difficult to see how the excellently phrased 'pursuit of happiness' can mean anything except the liberty to pursue that goal in your own way. It would be hard to see how the state could have a duty to provide your happiness. With the right to 'life' it is less clear whether what is required is non-interference by the state or the provision of a state health-service.

Whatever the origin of the term, in practice rights have become a politically enforceable contract with demands and expectations. Sometimes the contract seems to be rather one-sided. It is assumed that the basis of civilisation is that physiological existence as a human being by itself imposes on others the duty to do something about it. As a battle-cry (as in women's liberation movements) this is fine but once the obvious tyrannies have been removed the battle-cry is inadequate as an operating philosophy because rights without obligations is merely power-play. Just as freedom may need to be earned so rights need to be balanced by the second leg of the contract, that is by obligations. Obligations are, of course, no more than the receiving end of the rights demanded by others. The two should be so inseparable that a demand for one is always accompanied by a statement of the other.

Love

Love is a grossly inadequate translation of the second battle-cry of the French Revolution, for what seemed to be implied was brotherliness and comradeship. The word 'love' is used here because it enlarges the general concept.

The fellow feeling among members of a small group like a guerilla band is strong and wonderful. It can almost amount to love. Then there is a rather different feeling towards members of one's club or community. You may dislike certain individuals rather intensely but because they are members of your own group your treatment of them is different. In the future, society is probably going to have to make more use of this feeling with the smaller organisation units that every social seer demands – and which will be made technically possible by the computer.

In many countries politeness is the way you treat your friends. Yet the original basis of politeness, as also of Christian love, was the way you treated everyone. To some extent this concept of politeness still exists in Japan and the UK. It should be made clear that many other countries are more friendly but friendliness and politeness are quite distinct: friendliness is the readiness to accept someone on a superficially friendly basis; politeness is a readiness to behave in a certain way. The former is more attractive but the latter more reliable. The main trouble with group feeling or brotherliness within a group is that it so often does not extend outside that group and can even become hatred towards those outside the group. A white minority in a black country has a feeling of solidarity within the white community but, perhaps, racist discrimination outside it. By defining the group within which you are going to be brotherly you may be defining the rest of the world as the group which is not going to benefit from this attitude.

As I have mentioned in another book, I feel that the Christian concept of 'love' has inadvertently become counter-productive. As an ideal it is fine but as an operating principle it is unreliable. In a euphoria of Christianity it is probably possible to love your enemies but when the euphoria passes you are left with nothing. It should also be remembered that this exertion of brotherly love on your part was not for the benefit of your loved enemy or of society but for the benefit of your to-be-improved soul from which, through practice, hatred was to be expunged. So as long as you were *trying* this near impossible task that is what mattered. But other people would only benefit when you had *succeeded* in this impossible task. A rescue team may make heroic efforts to reach a stranded mountaineer but he only benefits when they actually reach him.

The result of the failure to be perfectly Christian in one's love of others is either abandonment of the hopeless task or the selection of one's own group who are somewhat easier to love.

I think we should keep this concept of brotherly love for all members of the human race because it leads to care and concern and with some people it fuels heroic altruism. But we badly need a 'two-tier system' so that if we cannot aspire to this considerable exercise of virtue we may still have an operating idiom that smooths the interactions of society. The obvious choice is respect. Respect for another person. Respect for the life space of another person. Not because he is a lovely person. Not because he is a member of your group. Not because you want something from him. Not because he is bigger and tougher than you. But because respect is a useful currency that ultimately benefits everyone.

In practice it is difficult to establish a respect for respect because it seems cold and bland and unexciting. It is not emotional or euphoric like love. It may need conscious rehabilitation. It may need to be part of a defined self-image.

Equality

'Equality' is marvellous as a battle-cry and as useful today as it was at the time of the French Revolution when there was so much inequality and privilege to sweep away. Paradoxically the word 'inequality' is not the opposite of 'equality' but equality is the absence of inequality. Just as the concept of freedom is really the absence of tyranny, so equality is the absence of (or objection to) inequality.

As an ideal a plain girl may resent the prettiness of some of her sisters (especially with divorce laws that can make a pretty girl a more effective money-earner than the most hardworking and talented executive). Because it is a fact of nature and no one's fault does not make her resentment unreasonable. She may choose to do something about it by increasing her skill in make-up or seeking to deny make-up facilities to the already pretty. Or she may put less of a value on beauty or even find a beholder who can appreciate her own variety of beauty.

That there are differences amongst people is undeniable. Some are short, some are tall, some are hard-working and some are lazy, some get high blood-pressure and some do not, some are beautiful and some are less beautiful, some are intelligent and some are less intelligent. The danger begins when we start using an apparently objective measure for special treatment. For example we may believe that height contributes to soldier-liness and insist on a minimum height for recruitment. This will look nice on the parade-ground but there is no evidence that the tall soldier is better in the battle-field. The success of the small Gurkhas and not so tall Scots might argue otherwise. We might suppose that apparently objective 'intelligence' tests could pick out the people who are going to be more effective at most things – since 'intelligence' is so basic a quality. Here we run into immense dangers because of our loose use of the word intelligence. If we call the test an 'xyz' test and find that those who do well at it also do well in certain occupations then that test may usefully predict recruits for that occupation. But to use the common currency of the word 'intelligent' is highly danger-ous. Most jobs require a mixture of intelligence, thinking skill, creativity, drive, effectiveness and reliability. The traditional IQ test measures just one of these and then seeks to discriminate on this basis.

Would we choose by lottery: a brain surgeon, a lawyer to defend us in court, a 5,000-metre runner for the Olympics, or the head of a factory? We might choose by lottery from amongst all those who were properly qualified. But we would not choose our brain surgeon by lottery from the street. Would it be good enough to choose a group of people from the street by lottery and then train them up to be brain surgeons? We might do reasonably well but would miss the great talent that was available in someone unchosen by the lottery. Just as in athletics we seek to develop the best and make no pretence about equality of talent so it makes sense in most areas to use the different talents.

The Cuban government is highly selective with regard to athletic ability and the chosen few are given special training, education and privileges. In Soviet Russia schoolchildren are early separated into special schools for the gifted. Communist party officials have special privileges as regards shopping, accommodation, cars and many other things. No party official and no politician who preaches equality considers that he himself has reached that position through a lottery system rather than through the exercise of his talents.

Nevertheless it is reasonable to be against one sort of privilege – of birth, of wealth, of capital, of class – in order to be in favour of another sort. It is useful to use the general battle-cry of equality in the battle stage.

Difficult as it may be to achieve, many people would be in favour of the sort of equality which lines people up at the beginning of the race so that they have an equal start. Equality of opportunity seems reasonable. It is when the race starts that the trouble begins. When the inequalities of stamina and stride start to show, some runners will lag behind the others. We can of course complain that this was because they were undernourished before the race or that the forward runners had private coaching. Some of this is probably true but nevertheless even when we equal out all these factors some runners are going to be faster. Do we hold back the faster runners? Or do we let them forge ahead and at the end of the race give them no greater prize than the others? If there is no reward are they going to make the effort? In real life, in a market economy, it is claimed that the reward success of the talented serves to raise the living standards of the less talented. Much depends on the distribution system for the created wealth. Holding back or punishing the talented seems to make no sense at all except as a slogan of envy. Failing to reward them seems to require from them a motivation which is unlikely to be widespread. Moreover we are looking not only at the motivation of those who have reached certain positions but the motivation of those who might have to work hard to reach them.

Rewards can be in honours or privileges as well as in money. Non-financial rewards for talent or effort are nothing new. They are also cheap. Their other advantage is that they are fixed and, unlike the reward of money, cannot be used to buy further privileges. Non-market rewards can also serve to keep people in line whilst they work towards these rewards – proper behaviour whilst you work towards a knighthood in the British Civil Service.

The real problem with the banner of equality is to know whether it is held aloft by motivations of envy, opportunity or gain. It can serve as camouflage for simple envy that someone else should have more talent or luck and as envy it is satisfied by removal of the cause. When the cry for equality arises from frustration at the lack of opportunity (for example in education) then the logical progression is that when opportunity is provided for the frustrated talent the talent should be able to blossom – in fact an equal chance to get in on the inequality race. In terms of gain a person is in favour of equality if he stands to gain, and against it if he stands to lose. As living standards rise the cry for equality will diminish because more people feel that they have something to lose from a levelling down. In material terms there can, of course, be no such thing as equality by levelling up. If we reduce equality to considerations of gain it becomes a power-play no different from any other.

Perhaps we should restrict the concept to equality of opportunity and equality of treatment. For the rest a balance is struck between the reward for effort and talent, and the contribution expected from it. That society should make the best use of the talents available to it must be in the best interests of society. More is expected from those who have more to give – but it is not confiscated.

Summary

I feel that the three battle-cries described in this chapter are fine as battle-cries but inadequate as constructing or operating principles with which to build a positive society. They had an immense usefulness at moments of revolution and change. They had a usefulness when protest against something was a powerful shaping force. They are still useful on a defensive basis. But I believe the potential that technological change has brought within reach can never be reached through attack and defence with day-to-day patching up in between. We need some positive constructing principles: some positive concepts to act not as battle-cries but as effort-focusing banners.

9 POSITIVE CONCEPTS

Many of the concepts described in this chapter will be elaborated or even repeated later when specific aspects of society are considered. As general concepts, however, they have a place here. There will be a great temptation to use that creativity-killing phrase 'the same as...' when a suggested concept comes near to one of our repertoire of concepts. For example Mussolini made the trains run on time so anyone who attaches importance to trains running on time is easily classified as a neo-fascist. I shall happily run that sort of risk rather than creep about in a CYA posture. At other times the problems that may arise from a concept may seem to outweigh the advantages. That is often because problems require less mental effort for their elucidation. Finally almost any concept if abused or taken to extremes can be dangerous.

Organisation

I do not think we have any choice at all in the matter of deciding that the priority concept of the future must be organisation. No one can deny that the world is becoming ever more complex and the only way of dealing with complexity is organisation. Fortunately the tool of the organisation revolution is to hand with the computer.

The concept of organisation terrifies most people because at once they think of an Orwellian state or a science-fiction computerised robot state. Both these are childish reactions and nursery battle-cries. Organisation and structure are not the enemy of freedom but the very fabric of it. Anyone who has anything at all to do with biology must marvel at the wonders of organisation. Unfortunately our history, misguided thinking, religious heritage and concept poverty has always painted organisation as repressive and dictatorial.

Without organisation there is only one sort of freedom: that is jungle freedom. Even that is probably a false analogy because those who have studied animals at close quarters know that they show a remarkable structure of social organisation. Let us say rather than without organisation there is no alternative to naked power-play. Of course this can be regulated to take the viciousness out of it but with the viciousness goes the vigour and the result is apathetic drift.

To enjoy watching a game of football you have to rely on the organisation of the game in terms of its rules; the organisation of the running of the game in terms of referee control and non-interference by spectators; the organisation that has built the stadium; perhaps the efforts of the police to control vandalism; the organisation of a transport system to get you to the stadium and away again; the organisation of a television network if you want to watch it at home; the organisation of satellite systems if you want to watch the World Cup in another country. If any of these organisations were faulty you would tend to get furious.

We fear organisation because we fear loss of individuality and being turned into robots. Organisation can certainly do that. But that is a wrong sort of organisation. Organisation can be used positively to increase individuality and freedom. That a knife can be used to kill does not keep it out of our kitchens where we use it in another way. Our quarrel is not with the concept of organisation but the use of that powerful device by incompetent thinkers and power maniacs. A simple organisation principle called 'flexitime' allows people to come to work and leave when they please. By any definition that must be an increase in freedom because if they wish they are still free to choose their usual hours.

Quite recently I had to travel from Cambridge to catch a plane at Heathrow airport. The journey takes about 90 minutes by train to London and then 40 minutes by underground to the airport. If the Cambridge train was over 30 minutes late on a 90 minute journey I would miss the plane. My experience of the trains was such that such a delay seemed likely (statistics could prove me wrong but that was my perception) so I felt that I had to take a taxi from Cambridge for the 75 miles to the airport. On the way back I had to travel by train from Locarno to Zürich and then on to Zürich airport. The train journey is over 3 hours and if the train had been more than 10 minutes late I would have missed the plane. But I had confidence in the Swiss trains. Although the train had to stop quite often because of alterations to the track, the train arrived in Zürich exactly on time to the minute. Does it really matter to society if trains run on time? Why should one always be in a hurry? There must be more important values than trains on time, mustn't there? The answer is that running the trains on time matters almost more than anything else in society. Unless we can take the basic fabric of society for granted then we are not free to do much else. It is difficult to see how sloppy or inefficient organisation has a positive value for anyone. If you have to telephone for an ambulance you want the telephones to work. If your house is burning down you expect the fire brigade to be efficient.

Efficient organisation will only happen if it is regarded as an end in itself. The fact that machines are accurate does not make accuracy an inhuman characteristic. You only have to watch a skilled craftsman exerting his human skill to know that. A good farmer will know when to plant to the day. A sloppy farmer will not try to blame his inefficiency on his greater humanity.

Envelope structures

Politically we tend to create a polarisation with individual freedom on the one hand and total state control on the other. The paradox of Marxism is that it set out to value individuality so highly that it has been felt necessary to abolish it in favour of State control, to the extent that licences may be required to move from one city to another. Yet the purpose of society is to set up frameworks ('envelopes') within which people can be more free, than ever. We cannot do this just by defending individual freedom whenever this is abused by the state. We need a positive effort to make sure that the envelope type of organisation is effected rather than the fishbone type in which every person is controlled from the centre. Design by protest is not good enough. If we fear organisation then, by default, it becomes the business of the state and that probably is fearful.

Our homes are 'envelopes' within which we are free. Our clubs and sports associations are organisational 'envelopes' within which we are free provided we abide by the agreed organisation structure. Our places of work are not yet coherent envelopes within which we can be free. That is an area which requires attention.

Organisation nodes and 'nodalism'

I would feel much freer if much of the hassle and complexity of modern life was delegated to an organisation centre – chosen by me – rather than treated as a transaction between the government and myself. If my tax affairs, loans, mortgages, insurance and all the other financial fabric of life were taken care of by one organisation 'node' this would be a significant addition to my freedom. It may be that eventually I would make purchases through that node, arrange health care and travel, possibly education and even marriage. Possibly my working services would be employed by that node which would hire me out on contract. I would expect life-time security of employment. All this is no more than a large Japanese company has always done for its employees in a sort of paternalism. Computers make the whole process quite easy. The node might organise group purchases of campers or boats or holiday homes which individuals might want to use but not own. There could be a physical club basis (like a stately home in the UK) or there need not be.

Is this suggestion related to paternalism or collectivism or feudalism or what? Is it perhaps a sort of *tribalism* in which a functional tribe is created and becomes a functional community? It is something of all these and that is why I have suggested the term 'nodalism' to emphasise its neutral organisational aspect.

The exact form and the mechanics of operation can easily be worked out – with provision built in for change and evolution. The nodes would not be government bodies though there might be agreed supervision as with the building societies. In time the government might deal directly with the nodes rather than with the individual through the node: for example the node might pay a lump tax bill which was then allocated by internal agreement amongst the members. There would be choice and provision for change but also some obligations to take a fair share of no-hopers and problem cases. In short the nodes could become internal 'alternative governments': community governments.

There is nothing revolutionary in the elements of the concept: we already have cooperatives, credit unions and condominiums as examples of group organisation. In six years, in the USA, cooperatives (in retail) have grown from 277 to over 1,000. In 1976 in the USA 29 per cent of pay was in the form of fringe benefits such as dental care plans and medical plans arranged by corporations for their employees.

Like the feudal barons of old the nodes would interpose a new layer of organisation between central government and individuals. But it would not be a power base except perhaps in terms of consumer action. If the node became the employer then it would work out employment contracts that would be honoured.

I would regard financial services as the most useful starting point for such nodes. This would allow a concrete starting point and area of convenience. As the concept developed then the community aspect could grow. The main thing is that it should be done on an efficient basis and provide a genuine increase in freedom, not that it should depend on community good-will and dedication, with low efficiency.

New professions

I think that, as part of the organisation priority, we need to design some new professions. There is no reason why we should be content with the existing ones which may have been adequate in a less complicated society centuries ago. In practical terms the nodes could act as an initial base for developing these professions.

The role of the social worker could be extended, solidified and given more status. There is always going to be need for the pastoral care of the weak, the unfortunate and the difficult. But it must be realised that social workers will always be fully occupied, with little time at all to cope with other people's less desperate problems. So a new profession would be that of general 'coper' or fixer. Such a person would be an information source and an operator – not unlike the courier on a package tour. He would know who to put people in contact with, how to locate information, how to do certain things, know about changes in the law and so on. If the social worker is a modern day evolution of the Italian parish priest the 'general coper' would be a modern day evolution of the small-town solicitor in the UK. Then there might be a 'general listener' or advisor. He, or she, would not be a psycho-analyst or a fixer but a combination of a good friend, a sympathetic doctor, a Samaritan and again the parish priest. Such a person would be chosen almost entirely on the basis of personality and motivation. Another possible profession would be that of the 'people-person' with a role reminiscent of the play leader, the entertainments officer on a cruise, the television host and the flight service director on a Jumbo jet. His personality would be different from that of the listener: he would be more gregarious and more extrovert. Again personality would be the main qualification.

An important profession would be that of the 'work-packager'. We assume that work to be done presents itself in neat packages but this is far from the case. The work-packager would 'design' work. He would seek out things that needed doing, put them together, coordinate needs, design the work according to the degree of skill of those who might be going to do it. There is an urgent need for the development of such a profession. The professional negotiator is another possibility who could be called in to organise negotiating frameworks rather than to help either side. The role of the 'money-doctor' – for every manner of financial advice – would fit naturally into the node. Leisure development needs a broader base than just a sports officer.

It may be argued that these roles are adequately covered by doctors, analysts, priests, lawyers, bank managers and voluntary workers. It may be argued that it would be wrong to take much of the human advice element away from these people. In practice, however, highly skilled professionals do not always have the time for the 'people care' suggested by these professions. Where would the people come from and how would they be paid? There is likely to be growing unemployment. There is likely to be a shedding of people from service organisations as automation takes over the routine jobs. Many people in society are at present unemployed because their personality talents do not have a natural niche. There are retired people who might excel at some of the jobs. A new source of labour will also be described later.

Payment would not be on a job basis but on a subscription basis – probably as part of the overheads of the node – in the same way as executives are paid in an organisation.

Computers are going to be so central to organisation in the future that there will probably develop a sort of computer 'doctor' who can be called in as required – or even a 'computer corps' independent of the manufacturers.

Simplicity

In 1949 in the USA there were 248 people employed by the state and local government for every 10,000 people in the population. By 1977 this had risen to 477. The passing of Proposition 13 in California means that pressure is on to simplify government because the electorate have given warning that increased taxation is going to be resisted. Simplicity should be a fundamental guideline for all organisation development. The purpose of the computer should not be to make complexity tolerable but to make simplicity possible. Simplicity should be the over-riding concept in the design of any system. Task-forces may need to be set up to simplify procedures, laws, tax systems, reporting systems and any other activity of this sort. Into every system should be built an evolutionary trend towards simplicity so that a system should itself suggest how it might be simplified.

Simplicity need not mean starkness or crudeness. Simplicity means working towards human values, human understanding and a robustness of systems. Complicated forms should be banned. It is bad architecture to design a highly complicated system so that abuse is difficult and exceptions are rare. It makes much more sense to design a simple system that will cope with the bulk of requirements with special procedures for coping with the exceptional case. Simplicity need not mean lack of flexibility.

Instead of government moving ahead with its own complexity and expecting everyone else to keep up, the onus is on government to simplify its procedures. Simplicity must be acknowledged as an operating principle that cannot be abandoned under any circumstances. Year by year an administrator should be asked to tell how he has succeeded in making his system simpler that year. It goes without saying that simplicity is not to be judged solely by the designer of the system but also by whoever is going to have to use it.

Effectiveness

The concept of effectiveness is not the same as the concept of efficiency. Efficiency is a ratio comparing input to output. Effectiveness is a decision that something must be designed and operated so that it will work. Effectiveness involves the best use of resources without waste. Effectiveness also involves priority decisions. Effectiveness involves finding the best way to do something and the taking of responsibility. Effectiveness involves the development of talent and the use of talent.

Of any organisation it should be said that it is simple and effective. Effectiveness involves close consideration of the people who are going to run the scheme and the people who are going to use it. Effectiveness is a practical concept, not a theoretical one. Compromise may be effective in solving a dispute of the moment but it usually has no sustained effectiveness in terms of finding the best way to do something.

It is very unlikely in the future that work will be an end in itself. For that reason an increasing emphasis will have to be placed on effectiveness. The purpose of productivity will be to produce time as well as material goods. Effectiveness may involve pragmatism but it is not concerned with expediency and ad hoc adjustments, since these are likely to be ineffective in the long run. Effectiveness means the achievement of the effect intended with the resources available. If skilled design cannot match the two and if more resources are not available, then the intended effect may have to be realistically altered. Executives and government officials will need to be made personally accountable at each level for the effectiveness of their operation. Simply occupying a seat and running the rules as they were written will not be enough. If a change is needed then there should be by-pass channels for that change to be sanctioned for a trial period. Hiding behind the inertia of a large organisation should not be acceptable.

Effectiveness is not the same as the Protestant work ethic or the Japanese work culture. There may be more value in re-designing the system and working only one hour a day than in leaving the system as it is and working sixteen hours a day: the willingness to work hard has a value; the ability to work effectively has a result.

Effectiveness depends very largely on the design both of goals and of methods, and in turn, these depend on priorities and the allocation of resources. The effectiveness of wartime action usually arises from the firmness of priority decisions. Trying to satisfy two objectives at once usually leads to failure to satisfy either effectively.

Contribution

For most people in the developed societies boredom and lack of purpose will replace deprivation and poverty as the major concern. Sports, hobbies, crafts, esoteric sects and 'me-improvement programmes' will mop up only a small part of the available talent, energy and motivation. When the working week shortens, when the working life shortens, and when the year may be divided into 'working months' and 'non-working months' there are going to be a lot of people with time on their hands.

When this is combined with a movement against big government and ever-increasing government expenditure, the scene is set for a new sort of contribution from people towards the running of society. It will not be enough to pay one's taxes and then sit back with the privilege of criticising what the government is doing. Going into politics as a politician cannot absorb many people and in any case in the future the role of politicians will probably change considerably. People will regard the running of society as a legitimate area for their surplus talents, energy and experience.

To some extent voluntary societies and charities do already get involved in helping to run society, either in a focused way (like looking after the aged or raising money for research into disease) or in piecemeal project work. What will be required in the future is a definite organisational structure that will make the most use of the energy available. Training and re-training may be involved to supplement amateur good-will where this is insufficient. A commitment will also be required rather than dabbling or dilettantism.

The work would not be paid. To begin with the option might be given to some people to pay their taxes in a skill contribution rather than in money. That would be the transitional state and would allow an organisation to develop. Ultimately a contribution in time and effort towards the running of society would be regarded as matter-of-factly as paying taxes is today. The conversion of taxes through a large bureaucracy into an inefficient use of funds will come to be regarded as antiquated, and as denying citizens the right to use their energies for the benefit of society (other than by voting occasionally, and protesting).

In the USA in 1978 two items make up 47 per cent of the budget : $118 billion is earmarked for defence and $119 billion is earmarked for benefits for the aged. Looking after the elderly is one obvious area where positive contribution is required.

The contribution would have to be organised and effective and free of the petty politics that bedevil voluntary organisations. The work would not be paid – it would be 'non-market-labour'. The society of the future will probably contain a whole structure for non-market-labour and the concept will be described in more detail later.

The concept of 'earned freedom' was discussed earlier. It was suggested that freedom had to be earned through a contribution. The currency with which freedom would be earned would not be ordinary money but a new concept of 'social currency' which could be earned – in advance if necessary – by a positive contribution to society. This would have several elements. There might be a national service period through which all youngsters would pass. For those who chose not to work in a society that did not require everyone to work, unemployment benefits would be earned by spending a few months each year contributing positively to society as part of the 'non-market-labour force'. Other privileges that society might have to offer would also be earned by a willingness to spend time and effort in earning the 'social currency'. For example a person who had not done well enough in examinations to get into university might work his way in on this basis by showing his determination. A proportion of places might be set aside for such candidates. Other elements would be the contribution of retired people, or people with surplus time, or motivated people.

In short there would be a definite framework for social contribution. In some cases there would be an expectancy and a requirement to contribute in this way (as the Swiss train for the army each year). In other cases, contributing in this way would enable a person to establish a social creditor to work off a debt to society as in minor crime. The third aspect would be the tapping of the energy and skill of those who wish to contribute anyway.

From an organisation point of view the concept of positive contribution is not difficult. At first there would be howls of protest at cheap labour or even forced labour and unions would protest the competition. But this negative 'edge' would have to be crossed with determination. Society cannot afford to back off from the use of the talent and energy available to it because at the transition stage it is likely to be to the disadvantage of one group.

In some cases the social contribution might consist of self-help groups like the Saemaul groups that are improving village life in South Korea, or the groups that are improving conditions in the *favelas* around Rio. In other cases the contribution would not necessarily be on one's own doorstep but might take the task-force form.

Choice

The society of the future will be able to contain many more options than at present. Some people may still enjoy working hard. Others may enjoy working to earn money to spend on the material things they find pleasurable. Others will want to work less and enjoy time and a simpler way of life. Instead of one mode being the accepted one and the rest being considered aberrant there will be room for all options: provided those taking up the options are prepared to accept the obligations as well as the freedoms of the chosen option.

The requirements for such a society of choice are: increased productivity so that man is freed from the burden of having to work flat out all the time; much better organisation to allow for the alternative life-styles; and a shift in social values. All three of these are happening or, in the case of organisation, are possible. I see nothing sinister about a person's background details being recorded on a computer just as a flight reservation is now recorded, so that he can have the utmost flexibility in his life-style. Such a system might be unfair on a few people and it might make deception much more difficult but with suitable over-rides and controls it is bound to happen. The 'nodes' mentioned earlier would be the obvious organisation points and since these would be run on a cooperative basis the sanctions would be greater than if they were run by government.

In such a plural society there would be space for the loner and for the activist, for the artist and for the teacher, for people who like doing things and for people who like dealing with other people. There would no longer be a drop-out concept because that would be an accepted life-style of choice – some social contribution would be expected in return for a small guaranteed income and safety-net services of health and education.

In such a choice system it would be possible to go to university at any time in one's life. It would be possible to change careers and to change life-styles.

Belonging to one particular function 'node' would not preclude belonging to other organisations just as at the moment a person may belong to a religious group, a sports club, a hobby association and a voluntary work group.

There would be freedom to choose much as there is freedom to become a soldier, a monk, an actress or an athlete today. In some cases it is merely a matter of choice and once the choice is made then the freedom is earned by accepting the discipline of the chosen life-style. In other cases there might be the opportunity to choose but if the required talents were lacking then the life-style might not be possible.

I can imagine someone choosing to work four months of the year and having an easy time – or doing his own thing – the remaining eight months. Someone else might want to work every day but in the morning only. Another person might want to work hard in the normal style but to retire at forty-five. A further person might work hard for two years and take the third year off.

There will be times when society may not be able to afford the free choices of everyone. For example once upon a time in the island of Jersey there had to be a law passed that prevented men from knitting. Everyone had found that he could earn more from knitting than from tilling the small farms – so no food was being grown. There might be queues, rationing systems and lottery systems for the choices. As far as possible the freedom to choose would have been earned with the 'social currency' mentioned earlier. A person who had done three years' work in social contribution would come ahead of someone who had done none.

Happiness

The quality of life and happiness are more important than anything else. The purpose of society is the quality of life for its citizens. The purpose of human life is happiness – or its 'pursuit' as the US Declaration of Independence puts it. I have dealt at length with the notion of happiness in a previous book (*The Happiness Purpose*). In a future society we may need to spend a great deal more attention on it without being deterred by the cry that to do anything about happiness is artificial and self-defeating. Passive distraction and self-indulgence or the pursuit of kicks may be ineffectual in the long run, requiring an escalation of effort for diminishing satisfaction. Like training for a sport or learning to play a musical instrument, a skill in happiness may require some application. There is nothing strange in that concept. In the East there are major philosophies that believe it may take several life-times of deliberate training in order to reach happiness.

The quality of life must be a priority. But it is not likely to be increased solely by negative protest: preventing change and development. This will remain an important aspect but positive action is also necessary. Preventing desecration of the country-side is important but so too is the positive restoration of city centres. The energy of developers and commercial interests can be harnessed instead of being automatically rejected. Self-help groups and the social contribution scheme mentioned earlier are important ingredients in the continued pressure for improvement in the quality of life. There will be times, however, when a future benefit requires an action that at the moment appears to go in the opposite direction. This problem has been discussed so often in this book that I will not repeat it here. Design will be of the highest importance: not just the design of objects but of systems and methods to take into account human needs: a straggly and untidy-looking village might be a better design than a geometrical leisure complex.

In our search for improvement in the quality of life we should not seek to turn the clock back but we can certainly learn from the past of the things that mattered and contributed to the quality of life. As in other areas the emphasis is on being positive, not on regret and complaint.

There are people who achieve the maximum satisfaction in doing things for others. In a sense their behaviour is still directed towards their own good which happens to be achieved in this way. In any case altruism need not be regarded as the sole route to happiness. We could characterise the three parallel 'goods' as: doing good for oneself, doing good for others, doing good for tomorrow. An attitude which keeps all three of these in mind at the same time could be called 'bonism' from the French and Latin roots. The three are not in a priority listing – all three must be satisfied at the same time.

The relationship of self-image to happiness is a most important one. Whether a new positive self-image concept will emerge or not cannot be said. It would be hard to create by deliberate effort, but if a general positive mood was encouraged then a positive self-image might emerge as a crystallisation of the mood.

Discipline

Discipline is a word with ugly connotations although 'self-discipline' has long been regarded as a prerequisite for achievement in athletics or in the arts. We may need to invent a new word rather than rehabilitate the old one. It would be difficult for a positive future to develop in an atmosphere of carefree vandalism, laziness, petty-minded bickering, the what-you-can-get-away-with ethic, apathy and despair. Through a constant sneering at its more ridiculous excesses the concept of discipline has come to be regarded as an interference with humanity. This is largely by people who feel they have more to gain than to lose by its devaluation. Society, as a whole, may in time come to feel the opposite. Unless we wish to be forced into a switch from anarchy to fascism – supported by the timid who see it as their only hope of survival – it may be better to be positive about discipline and clear about our concept of freedom.

Summary

In this chapter I have sought to focus attention on the positive concepts that will lead to a positive future. The one I have not mentioned is 'thinking'. We are going to have to do a lot of focused thinking: thinking in a constructive way and attempting to design the future that we want. As I wrote at the start of the book the quality of our future is going to depend on the quality of our thinking, whether we like it or not. We shall have to overcome the CYA attitude which makes us terrified of saying anything that can be attacked. We must learn to design systems which, once started, acquire a momentum and effectiveness of their own. We ought not to be frightened of words like 'organisation' or 'discipline'. It is only too easy to howl with outrage at their mention and to conjure up examples of their abuse. We must overcome our love of the policy that 'doing nothing' is best because then there is no blame, no hassle, no possibility of making terrible mistakes. We do need to be ultra-careful but we also need to be positive, otherwise we waste the enormous opportunities that technology is about to offer us.

10 MOOD

In the end society depends on the mood of its people. In medicine there is the concept of reactive depression and endogenous depression. Reactive depression is supposed to be when a healthy person is depressed by her surroundings, by bereavements, by strains put upon her, and by misfortune of any sort. Endogenous depression, in contrast, is supposed to come from inside and to be due to chemical changes in the brain which are not a reaction to outside events. As we begin to learn more about the biochemistry of the brain we find that the distinction between the two may have some pragmatic value but that the overlap is considerable. Changes in brain chemicals may be caused by events, or these changes may occur spontaneously. The balance of chemicals is different in different people and some are more 'robust' than others. In truth we are almost back to the ancient Greek idea that moods were caused by different combinations of certain 'fluids' (humours) that perfused the body: hence 'melancholy' was due to black bile.

We can apply the same concepts of mood to society. Much of the mood of society is due to events and much to more general features like morale, lack of faith in politicians, violence, inflation and so on. Of course a mood in one person becomes an external event for everyone around, and so moods spread.

But there is a growing feeling that it is not just a series of events and that if these changed the mood of people would change. There is a growing feeling, proposed for example by Professor Ivor Mills of Cambridge University, that some basic features of society cause profound mood changes. For example overcrowding in animals causes changes in the glands leading to a drop in fertility and an increase in aggression. In depressed women there can be profound glandular changes caused as a result of the depression. We do know that the whole chemical regulation of the brain, of mood and of the glands is closely interconnected. Professor Mills has been particularly interested in the problems of coping. Society may simply be growing too complex for people to cope, and the result of this failure to cope is a change in the brain's chemicals followed by depression.

In 1975 the health service in the UK spent £12,063,000 on anti-depressants. One in every six women and one in every nine men will need psychiatric help in the course of her or his life. Depression occupies the time and attention of most general practitioners.

There seems to be an urgent need to do something about the complexity of life. Paradoxically it also becomes a mixture of boredom and complexity because in a complex society doing nothing is not peace but boredom. As aids to coping we use such things as alcohol (which is showing a rising consumption in almost all developed countries), the caffeine in coffee and Coca-Cola, the nicotine in cigarettes, and prescribed medicines. Three thousand tons of marijuana are imported into the United States from Mexico every year, quite apart from other sources of supply.

So in the future we will have to look not only at the cultural determinants of mood – which will still remain important – but also at the mechanical determinants such as the complexity of the world around us.

Television

By the time he is twenty the average youngster in the United Kingdom will have spent the equivalent of eight full working years watching television. That is assuming he watches no television until the age of five. The amount is quite staggering.

We have no idea what television viewing for hours on end does to the brain chemicals. The continued stimulation may facilitate the production of certain chemicals and in turn this may bring about the production of an increased amount of the 'inhibitory' or balancing chemicals. This would mean that when the stimulus was not acting there would be an excess of the 'downer' type chemical with depression and apathy. At the same time there would be aggression and irritability and a search for excitement that would again produce the 'upper' or stimulant effect. All this is largely unknown territory and there is much speculation, but from what we do know, something of the sort may well happen. The overall result would be depression, apathy and a search for excitement such as that produced by violence. We suspect that the brain becomes internally 'addicted' to its own chemicals – those that produce 'highs'.

Quite apart from these chemical effects the sheer passivity of television results in general passivity, lack of involvement, lack of the habit of achievement (as through a hobby or craft) and perhaps lack of proper development of the 'will'. By 'will' I mean the developed intention to do something as distinct from just reacting.

There is also the undeniable fact that those eight working years spent watching television would otherwise have been spent doing other things (perhaps worse, perhaps better). On balance, does the amazing educational and exposure value of television, which can bring to the meanest home experiences otherwise reserved only for the super-rich, outweigh the harm?

All the effects listed above are to do with the mechanics of television and are quite independent of the content. Much has been written and said about the effect of violence and the consensus of research indicates that television violence does seem to increase aggression and general violence. It could be a general effect on aggression. It could be straight imitation. It could be a de-sensitising effect so that the threshold into violence is much lowered. It could also be a change in the attitude to law and order, since the television heroes are usually cast in the loner role, relying more on purity of heart than on adherence to the law. Many of the possible remedies are in the hands of the consumer: for example an indefinite boycott of all products advertised in association with violent programmes. That would strike terror into the hearts of programme producers because negative advertising, once set off, might take years to recover from.

Jungle or nursery

Noble beasts stalk through the jungle free to express their potential and make their own way. Their power is their protection. They owe nothing to the jungle. Survival is the name of the game. What is offered is taken. Let the weak scurry away. For some this is their view of society. Society is a jungle landscape featuring regulations, people, institutions, governments and all the other vegetation. You travel light and boldly, taking what you can. The ethic is 'what you can get away with'. If you are caught or thwarted you shrug and move on. There is no sense of responsibility. Let everyone look after themselves. Nor is there any need to change society. You find your way by your wits through the jungle, you do not seek to improve it – improve it in what direction? The 'rip-off' ethic is smart and clever. A lion does not stand dutifully in a queue in order to make its kill.

The other idiom is that of the nursery. Children did not ask to be born. They are being 'exploited' anyway because someone – the parents – are indulging their need to have children. Children owe nothing. The purpose of childhood is to have the maximum amount of fun. There is always time to get serious later. The idiom is different from the jungle idiom because, of course, children are owed a great deal by their parents. They are owed affection, food, shelter and entertainment. It is the right of children to expect these things – not in exchange for accepting certain obligations but because they *exist* as children. If the 'goodies' are not forthcoming then there are sulks and rebelliousness and even violent demands. For parents we can read 'them', government, society in general. There is not even a sense of responsibility to oneself as there is in the jungle idiom (where you survive on your wits or die quietly) because if you are unhappy or in trouble then your parents owe it to you to rescue you.

Reflection heroes

Literature and art have for decades indulged in anguished self-examination until every pimple on the soul has been squeezed and picked at. The dominant fashion in art has become intensely self-centred: the artist has to tell the world every nuance of his feeling, every whisper of his libido. The reviewers and the critics want more and more detail, closer close-ups. This, they tell themselves, is really what life is about. This is not romanticizing – this is where it is at. There is an obsession with apparent truth, especially if that truth is anguished or sordid. Passions are noble just because they are passionate. Pop stars sing of the loves and anxieties which everyone imagines to be his own. A hero is someone who has as many pimples as you but bigger ones and ones he is not shy about exhibiting. It is the mirror ethic of art. In time people may get as bored with it as a schoolboy does with his first microscope after he has subjected everything at hand to its intense scrutiny.

As a result of this idiom many people make as careful and as detailed a production of their own souls as any theatrical director makes of a play. The lighting is changed, the words are changed – surely this production is worthy of an audience. Anguish is manufactured by expectations. A person at an encounter group who cannot break down into tears like the others, feels that unlike their warm human souls he has merely a transparent acrylic device.

Heroes are not super-heroes carried away by the nobility of their mission. Nor are they robust people striding through life taking things as they come and finding time to eat, drink and have a laugh. Why fish in the sea if you can make an aquarium of your soul?

It may be that once art has discovered that some mirrors are distorting mirrors and produce grotesque images which bear little resemblance to reality, it will find a more positive concept to follow. Should we then expect love stories between tractors in the manner of Russian or Chinese art or the romance of a laser-implosion mission?

The protest movement

Much has been achieved by the protest movement. Man has become more conscious – just in time – in his duty to the environment. Man has become more conscious of his duty to his fellow human beings. The quality of life has been shown to be more important than an accumulation of material goods. The change of mood is remarkable. And it has been brought about by dedicated and committed protesters. Long may they act as the conscience of society.

But protest by itself is not enough because positive construction is needed. It is too easy to wear a badge of protest and regard that as a sufficient contribution to society. Nor is working to put right the grievance a sufficient idiom because correction of faults – though necessary – is not sufficient for design.

As a result of the protest ethic young people tend to be anti-business, anti-material goods, anti-government, anti-politicians, anti-routine and anti- many other things. There is a noble yearning for the idyllic, simple life of a small community of happy, relating, people. Who could quarrel with that? The only dispute is whether it is best to work towards such ideals by working towards them or by being against everything else. We may need to build the frameworks within which that sort of choice will be possible.

Group idiom

Outsiders exist not as lone rangers but as bands of outlaws. Avant-garde trend-setters band together like surfers on the same wave. Individual ideas are suspect because 'ego-trip' has joined the other sneer expressions. Groups are cemented together more by their common enemies than by their common interests. Like soldiers in an Omdurman square they come together to let off synchronised volleys of sneers at the hordes around (dull, square, middle-class, privileged, etc.). There is no change here. To be fair the genuine trend-setters may indeed be individuals but the media speed so quickly equips them with a crowd of followers that the original individual is lost amid the group idiom.

Positive ideals

On the positive side there is an immense amount of good. Young people are more idealistic then ever. They do care more about other people and about the world in general. When the Laker sky-train from London to New York was over-popular the long queues of young people organised themselves superbly and waited cheerfully. There is less hypocrisy, and more concern for human values. Many people are yearning for a purpose in life to harness their energies and motivation. There is an apathy of futility because government seems so remote and so corrupt (because of a natural media focus on that), and there appears no channel for effort. People do want to be people. The rip-off artists, the self-indulgent and the jungle cats are no doubt in a minority but a trend-setting minority – for lack of any other trend.

Summary

Does mood follow situation or does mood create situation? Both happen. There may be very dangerous effects of modern society that threaten to change the mood of the people permanently quite apart from what is happening within society. That would be a very serious matter because we cannot proceed into the future as chemically doped zombies. Many idioms such as the protest idiom and the 'reflection' cult of art have probably passed their peak of usefulness and need supplementing with something more positive. The jungle ethic and the nursery ethic are both a danger to society. Against them can be set an increase in idealism and caring which at present lacks focus and structure.

11 PRODUCTIVE WEALTH

Anyone who lives in a developed country almost certainly owes his privileged position of comfort to the colossal increase in agricultural productivity over the last two hundred years. It takes one man to produce what hitherto had required one thousand. The rest can be employed in making other things or providing the services that we think we require.

Any consideration of a positive future must take a look at the problem of productive wealth and growth. Is growth desirable? Do we have to keep growing to survive? Do we need more material goods? What is it all about anyway?

Since the introduction of parking meters into the UK motorists have spent about £52 million on the meters. This has not gone to provide off-street parking but to pay for the maintenance of the service. Is that a waste? No, because we could say that the better regulation of traffic in cities has added to the quality of life and perhaps improved industrial productivity. Suppose we had come up with a brilliant concept (quite easy, really) which would have had the same effect of regulating traffic but required no expensive meters or maintenance? The motorists would have had that £52 million to spend in other ways on improving their quality of life. So they would have benefited doubly: the better traffic flow and the money to spend. That is the purpose of thinking, of concepts and of productivity. But what about the unemployed meter-makers and meter-maids? They should have been employed on something more productive. But what about unemployment and the creation of jobs?

In 1950 the National Health Service in the UK cost £500 million, in 1977 it cost £6,500 million. Part of this is due to inflation but health costs have rocketed and will continue to rocket as there are more drugs, more tests and more procedures that are possible. Of course there is a good deal of waste: 150,000 tonsillectomies a year are carried out and it is estimated that of these only 8 per cent are required. Waste of this or bigger orders of magnitude is not always anyone's fault. It is part of the uncertainty of medicine and the sheer continuity of some of its habits. There is probably a lot of money wasted on research like the £10 million a year spent on cancer research without finding any cure. But in 1975 the cost of treatment prescribed for peptic ulcers alone was £10,095,000, so how much would you spend on research into this area in order to save that money? Or would research only increase the cost by discovering a new and expensive drug which then became essential because every patient would have the right to receive it?

So there is spending on the things we consider to be part of the quality of life. There are 476,000 teachers in the UK and they have to be paid. Very nearly as many postal workers also have to be paid to provide another service that maintains the fabric of life. For our convenience there are 473,000 shops (1971 figure) employing 2,541,000 people. If we could do without those shops we could save a lot of money and employ all those people more usefully elsewhere.

In Canada a fisherman gets a mark-up of 48 per cent on his catch of sock-eye salmon and makes a profit of 7.08 per cent on sales. Next in line, the fish products company that cans it so that you can keep it on shelves and distribute it more easily gets a mark-up of 22.4 per cent and a profit of 5.36 per cent on sales. Then comes the wholesaler with a mark-up of 10.6 per cent and a profit of 1.26 per cent. Finally the food shop with a mark-up of 17.7 per cent and a profit of only 1.01 per cent. So you pay for the convenience of having salmon caught, canned, distributed and sold to you. If you grow your own first class protein from yeasts in tanks in the kitchen you will save an awful lot of money but miss that aspect of the quality of life that allows you to enjoy salmon. And all the salmon fishers will be out of a job (if others think like you).

So convenience and the other services we take for granted cost money. Of course there may be wastage and of course we do not have much say in how the money is spent (for instance in government). If we had options we might decide that other things were more important to our personal design for the quality of life – for example spending on a symphony orchestra rather than on research into strokes.

The quality of life is fuelled by our productive wealth. The purpose of our productivity is to produce three things: goods, services and time. By providing the same goods and services in less time, then we should, in the future, have more time to spend on other things.

Let us suppose there is value in digging a ditch – perhaps it is for an irrigation channel. Ten men set out to dig the ditch, each with a spade. It takes them three days. One day someone designs a ditch-digging machine with the result that one man using the machine can dig the same ditch in three days. That seems fine but it means that nine men are unemployed. So the nine men sit around with time on their hands and the one man digs the ditch. Or they can share the work round working in short shifts. At the end of the contract money for digging the ditch is shared around. Or those other nine men could each have built a machine and gone off to dig nine other ditches (supposing there is an unending demand for ditches). Or they could have sat around carving beautiful objects or spent time in their gardens or studying. It is by no means as simple as that because productivity is a complex system with market problems, edge effects, ratchet effects of expectancy, distribution problems and, of course, the capital problem of buying the ditch-digger. But it does not seem to make too much sense to say to the men: 'put aside the ditch-digger because you will then be unemployed and will be unable to find use for the time on your hands'. Nor does it make sense to ask that they do nothing else or they will lose their share out of the ditch-digging proceeds. Yet with our concept of unemployment we do both those things.

In many of the situations mentioned earlier the final problem was that of the people who would be thrown out of work (the meter-maids, etc.) by a change in concept or a change in needs. That edge effect is so powerful that it dominates our total economic thinking. If you are unemployed then unemployment happens to you one hundred per cent – not the 5 per cent that might be quoted in the papers. Actual unemployment or feared unemployment loses governments votes. Teen-age unemployment can lead to violence and the failure to acquire work habits. Also, on a Keynesian basis, the wages paid are used for consumption and so spur further manufacture which in turn increases employment which in turn increases consumption and so on.

Colin Leicester of the Institute of Manpower Studies at Sussex University reckons that with the expected growth in gross national product and the growth in labour force, by the year 2000 there will be about 5 million people unemployed in the UK (compared to about 1.5 million at the moment and about 5.6 million in the whole of the Common Market at the time of writing). He also estimates that by 1990 only one third of the work force will be employed in primary and secondary industry.

Let us make the problem even worse. We know that between 1951 and 1977 employment in agriculture fell from 5 per cent (of the working population) to 2 per cent; employment in manufacturing fell from 50 per cent to 40 per cent; employment in the service industries rose from 46 per cent to 58 per cent. We know that even in manufacturing industry up to a third of the workers are not concerned with production at all but are in offices. In fact one quarter of the total work force is at the moment employed in offices.

Now with the use of the cheap computers and some applied thinking we could probably reduce by three quarters the number of people actually employed in offices. So that could throw a further 18.75 per cent of the total work force out of work. Of course it would not happen but it would mean that they were employed in the same fashion as the nine men using spades because there was no other way to occupy their time. If I was a politician or an economist I would be horrified by these figures – and rightly so. But as a thinker one is inclined to look at the tremendous productive talent released to further improve the quality of life – if only we could find a way to use it effectively. And if only we could overcome the 'edge effect' of unemployment. For example the National Enterprise Board has had to prop up British Leyland cars with £246.5 million in cash and a further £100 million in loans because it could not be allowed to collapse.

Working for the sake of working may be good for your soul and may keep you out of mischief and these are both entirely valid reasons for working. Running up and down a mountain or digging and filling in holes are both labour, but beyond the good they do you they do not produce quality of life improvements for other people or provide you with a means of buying what you require. Making cars inefficiently at a high cost or ones so badly designed that consumers prefer imported cars is not very different except that you can force the consumers in your own country to buy them and so subsidise you. The slogan 'from each according to his ability and to each according to his needs' is socially attractive but it does make the assumption that the ability is exerted fully. 'To each according to his contribution' would make more sense since it might tie to the person the rewards of his effectiveness or lack of it. It would, however, be unfair on those who were unable to make a contribution because society had not yet designed situations in which they would contribute (a task for the 'work-packaging' profession mentioned earlier).

In Italy 13.5 million state pensions absorb about 11 per cent of the GNP. Pensions, like unemployment pay, are attempts to distribute to the non-productive the value that has been created by the productive. In 1976 for every economically active person in Italy there were 2.8 inactive people, in Germany 2.3, in France 2.4 and in the UK 2.1. It may be that in future these figures could rise to 3 or even 4 as employed workers aided by technology were able to support the others.

The wage content of the added value in shipbuilding is 78.8 per cent, in textiles it is 61.4 per cent and in the petroleum industry it is 15.5 per cent (since nature did most of the work millions of years ago and machines can do most of the rest).

The problem is not one of unemployment but of employment. The problem is indeed that of 'fear of unemployment' because our thinking has been so very poor in anticipating the problem and hoping that the policy of doing nothing together with crisis management will be enough. Ad hoc remedies and political expediency are never going to be enough. We need to think on three levels: ways to iron out fluctuations; design of economic systems that will sustain productive growth; change in our basic concepts of contribution, work and employment. The poverty of our thinking is best illustrated by the fact that there are many things that do need doing in society and many people out of work but the two cannot be brought together.

In a later section I shall discuss possible changes in our concept of work.

Summary

I do not think we can draw back from the concept of productive wealth. This wealth need not be in material goods but it can be in time, in services and in any desired aspect of the quality of life. We need productive wealth to fuel freedom. It is extraordinary that when technological advances promise to free man from the tyranny of continuous work we should be horrified at the problem of unemployment. The problem is an opportunity. Of course we have to do a great deal of focused thinking about it. But it does illustrate, perhaps better than anything else, the limitations of the policy of evolutionary muddle through and the difficulty of the edge effect.

12 WORK AND EMPLOYMENT

Our traditional concept of work is that you point someone in a direction and he keeps going flat out, and that is work. It is then the function of management to indicate the direction and to derive value from the invested effort. Work is our means of creating productive wealth and distributing it. A refrigerator is not a device for keeping food cool but a device for re-distributing the surplus wealth from the person who can afford to buy it to the man who makes it.

For a couple with two children about 8 per cent of spending goes on drink, tobacco and entertainment; about 35 per cent on food and clothing; about 39 per cent on housing, transport and services. The purpose of work is to pay for those requirements. If most of those were provided on a non-market basis (as in the feudal tied cottage system) the money requirement would be lower. If two families shared a house and transport the expenses might come down by almost 20 per cent.

As the hippies discovered, the need to work is directly proportional to the tailoring of one's requirements. The concept of total or continuous work for everyone may not be possible or desirable in the future. How then are work and non-work to be shared out? The standard methods for sharing out work include early retirement, prolonged education and the cutting of overtime. The Department of Employment calculated that if all overtime were cut there would be no unemployment in the manufacturing sector. This is, of course, mythical since much overtime is in maintenance and service sections and so cannot be shared out as an ordinary job. In addition the flexibility of overtime cannot be matched by hiring and firing.

We should perhaps be looking at different levels of unemployment. The first level is where unemployment affects a small minority of people – but amongst youngsters and amongst the disadvantaged such as the blacks in some towns the rate may approach 30 or even 50 per cent. The next level is where unemployment affects a large minority. The third level is where it is a way of life for half or more of the population. Clearly the latter two levels are some way into the future. But there is no reason why we should not set up concepts and structures now.

The first stage might be to create structures for those who do not wish to work full time and who prefer to work half the time and to live a simple life. For example we might have two-day jobs or half-day jobs. There is a danger that these would suck in housewives and others who are at the moment outside the labour force – but they will probably be coming in sooner or later anyway. There could be the concept of the split job, where two people jointly occupied the job and decided between themselves who was going to work and when. The concept of temporary secretaries is well established as is that of locum doctors or teachers. In all these cases people work for a short length of time and then go on holiday or leave to pursue some hobby. We should aim to make this partial work much more accessible – on the basis that it could release full time jobs for others with different desires.

In the 'nodal' concept discussed earlier people might be employed by their 'node' and earnings would then be shared out according to the contribution of the individuals. The concept of 'people-employers' is already well under way with

organisations such as 'Manpower' which hires out temporary office workers as required. The 'node' concept might
have more of the flavour of the community where those
who were working paid their earnings into a kitty for the
common benefit.

There is a further concept: non-market-labour (NML). It
seems absurd that if unemployment benefits are to be paid
anyway then no use is made of the productive skills of those
who – through no fault of their own – are being subsidised
by the rest of the community. The idea would be to create
an NML sector which would be involved in activities which
were not by themselves economically viable but which greatly
increased the quality of life for others. Such projects might
include leisure developments, care of the aged, cleaning-up
projects, transport, house building, crime-prevention and
many other tasks that could be taken over. The NML sector
would provide a structure for the social contributions mentioned in a previous chapter. It could provide a structure for
a sort of national service that youngsters might be expected
to go through on leaving school. Anyone on unemployment
benefits might be expected to spend some time with the
NML sector. In one form the idea is not dissimilar to the one
used by Dom Mintoff, the Prime Minister of Malta. From a
psychological point of view it gives something to do, achievement, mateship and the continuance of the work discipline.
There might even be those who preferred to spend a few
months each year in the NML and take the rest of the time
off. Of course the idea would be strongly resented by some
unions who would see it as taking over their work. Fixed salaries would be paid and no tax would be payable. Though on
a rather larger scale, the concept is related to the kibbutzim
in Israel. The NML sector would act both as a task force for
getting things done and as a cushion for employment fluctuations. In essence the NML would be a sort of non-military

army. It could even be run by the Services. An immediate suggestion would be that such an organisation would be rather like slave labour. But it would be no more like slave labour than the existing civil service who are paid salaries to do specific jobs. The NML workers would be paid salaries anyway and then work would be found. A good parallel might be the war-time Land Army.

Up to a point it must seem to make more sense to keep on the unnecessary workers in British Steel, and to accept losses of £500 million a year (about 20 per cent of all central and local government borrowing), than to dismiss the 44,000 men and then have the task of doing something with them.

But we know, by definition, that those men are not contributing to the steel production and may actually be making it less productive than if they were not there. An acceptable NML sector working within the economy could provide a positive direction for the gradual solution of such problems. NML would be public sector employment on a corps basis rather than an individual basis.

In the future we may come to accept several different tiers of employment. There might be employment as we know it today. Then there would be a tier of moonlighting or DIY employment in which people learn a trade or skill and then practise it in their own time and usually for ready cash. Some formalisation of this may be useful – for example exemption from income tax but payment of an annual licence fee for registration, which fee would also cover insurance for the customer in case the new plumbing broke down. This would simplify tax collection and increase work incentive. Next a tier of casual workers or temporary workers or part-time workers who have no wish and no need to work full time. The NML sector would then have its share of workers. The 'node' organisations or people-employment-companies would employ people and offer package services on contract. The concept of people employment will be considered later.

To make any of these concepts possible there would have to be changes in organisations and in administration concepts.

Work design

There is one tax collector for every 900 tax payers in the UK and there is one general practitioner for about every 3,000 patients. So we could double the number of doctors by reducing the tax collection staff by between a third and a quarter. Which profession is the more productive? It is not easy to say. The doctor may save a few lives or may patch up people who are never going to be economically active whereas the tax man collects the funds that pay for the government and keep the framework of the country in repair so that economic productivity can go on. On the other hand even if you never need a doctor his availability is an insurance that adds to your quality of life. And if you had to save large sums of money just in case you had to pay high doctor's bills then your standard of life might go down. But your money saved for this purpose would be available to fuel industry just as the very high savings rate of the Japanese (who have little welfare service) provided investment capital for Japanese industry.

There are activities which have an amplifying effect, for example creating a park which many people might enjoy; and others which are only for your own benefit – like subsistence farming. There are others which are productivity 'sinks' inasmuch as they absorb wealth and just drain it away: for example paper-pushing in large bureaucracies requires the payment of several salaries and at the end there may be nothing to show for it except a system that runs itself but is of little use to anyone else.

The area of work design is going to have to develop as an area of huge importance. There will be work packaging; the design of work to fit available skills; the design of work so that it can be done by temporary workers who change frequently; the creation of value-adding tasks; the design of enjoyable jobs and the design of achievement.

Strikes

Many more days are actually lost through rheumatism and through casual absenteeism than through publicised strikes. What is surprising is not that strikes are used irresponsibly but that they are used so responsibly considering what an immensely powerful weapon they are. As society grows more complex everyone depends on everyone else. A few toolmakers on strike can bring a large car factory to a halt. The strike of key computer people can paralyse local government. Hospital porters on strike can dictate the policy of the Department of Health. French air-traffic controllers on strike can wreck the holidays of thousands of people in the UK.

In 1977 supermarkets started to sell low price loaves when the limit on the discount at which bakers could negotiate with shopkeepers was removed. The bread delivery men struck and refused to deliver bread because they felt the low prices would drive out the small shops and bakeries and so reduce their own jobs.

A key group of nineteen civil servants protested at the spending cuts in the Department of Employment (which employs 51,600 people) and refused to process the statistics the government needs for its economic planning.

Aero-engines sent from Chile to Britain for repair are held up for years because the workers do not approve of the regime in Chile.

Key groups of people have the power to influence political decisions through leverage. They institute strike action, if they are suspended then the confrontation begins and solidarity spreads the strike.

The logic of strikes is inexorable at each stage. Once strikes are effective in raising pay they become essential because pay will not be altered unless pressure is exerted by a strike. A union leader at a lower level sees confrontation as the logic of his job, his way to measure achievement and maintain his support. A powerful union asks for a wage rise to cover both inflation that has already occurred and anticipated inflation. This encourages other claims. In the end the wage claims help to exacerbate inflation. Those with less powerful unions, or less power, fall behind. In effect wealth is transferred from the weak to the strong. At each stage – as in most positive feed-back systems – we can see that logic dictates a course of action.

In general responsible union leadership has been effective in keeping wage claims within the region of pay guidelines. The problem is more that of wild-cat strikes and local disputes. Once the strike habit has been acquired – as at British Leyland or the Chrysler Linwood plant – it is difficult to put it away again.

From the companies' point of view it often makes economic sense to pay off the strikers rather than prolong the strike. The cost is simply passed on to the consumer. In times of pay restraint differentials are eroded so the skilled workers then strike to restore differentials. A compromise – as in the manning disputes in the newspaper industry – can make sense at the moment but lead to fatal inefficiency later. On many occasions a corporation has been closed down permanently by a strike, so losing the strikers both their claim and their jobs. On other occasions the workers know that in the end the government will step in to preserve jobs if necessary.

Is there a solution short of confrontation on a chosen battle-field? Many people feel that the mood may be changing and that workers realise that it is no longer the workforce against greedy capitalist management but one group of workers exerting its power at the expense of another group. When a small section of a company goes on strike the workers in the other sections suffer. The realities of economic life are also coming through. Raising prices and lowering productivity may mean pricing oneself out of the market. Real wage-increases are obtained more by productivity increases than by artificial wage-rises. Tariff barriers and government investment cannot protect an industry that is intent on suicide. Small groups of political activists are not using the unions to benefit the workers but to further their political beliefs.

The moment may soon come when the unions accept a larger role as the organisers of labour rather than as the organisers only of protest.

Summary

In this chapter I have suggested two broad concepts. The first is that of work sharing which can be done in a number of different ways. We can formally recognise that some people wish to work less and use less money. We should have structures to accommodate them and their chosen life-style. We can also create a variety of job structures other than full time jobs. We can seek to share work through employment by a people-employing agency or the organisation nodes mentioned earlier. The transactions of the future may no longer be between individuals and employers but between one employer and another.

If people are given a chance to spend their money on what they perceive as valuable service then they may be more efficient at *creating* these new values than is the government who would otherwise take the money as taxes. Suppose a group of elderly ladies clubbed together to employ a joint driver to drive them into town for shopping. That would be a job created.

The second broad concept is that of non-market-labour which would work to increase the quality of life in a community on a basis that would not be possible in terms of market values. If ten unemployed people were helped to create a leisure park that would be additional value and at little more cost (materials) than their unemployment benefits. As a sort of land army the NML might in itself attract people who wanted a definite structure to work within, and companies to work with.

13 INDUSTRY AND CAPITAL

In many of the developed countries other than the United States few traditional capitalists remain. The major holders of capital are the pension funds and the financial institutions such as the insurance companies. In the UK the British Railways pension fund is a major buyer of art. So many of the old battle-cries directed against greedy and exploiting capitalists are pointless today.

The distinction is not often made between the ownership of capital and the 'decision ownership' of capital. The former refers to an asset that can be sold at a price. The latter refers to a person who has the right to make decisions regarding the use of the capital but does not own it to sell. The chief executive and chairmen of large companies are in this position. It is claimed that such people although not owning the capital have to be sensitive to the shareholder owners either directly or through a stock market valuation.

Death duties, estate duties or capital transfer tax are designed to remove capital from those who have it and to distribute it via the government to everyone else. But the whole purpose of capital is to create productive wealth and the distribution of capital in tiny amounts kills the productivity. Dismantling a small business simply causes the production value of that business to disappear. We could, if we wished, separate the ownership of capital from its productive use by following the Roman law concept of 'usufruct' whereby a person has the right to use the capital as his own but not the right to sell it. It is therefore much in his interest to make it work productively and in so doing he creates employment and productive wealth. In short we are back to the manager. Most economists, except those who need a slogan, have long since realised that the capitalist society has been replaced by the managerial society.

What people are not so sure about is for whose benefit the manager exerts his talents. In the first place it is obviously for his own benefit and sense of achievement as a manager – he wants to run a successful enterprise and profits are the traditional measure of success. But in the second place is it the interests of the shareholder, or the work-force, or the consumer? Outside a monopoly situation the interests of the shareholders and consumers are quite well aligned insofar as the consumer exerts his buying preference. The consumer does, however, need protection against unsafe merchandise whose faults he cannot detect at once or even later. Where the work-force receives a fair share of the added value then their interests would also seem to be protected except that new machinery can displace workers, and investment decisions may shift work from one plant to another. Provided the investors are using their capital productively then the quarrel, if it arises at all, would seem to be between the productive use of capital, the interests of a particular group of workers, and the consumer. By and large the unions in the USA have been less defensive than those in the UK and they have chosen to share in real growth rather than to defend their position and impede growth. It seems unfair that a hard-working labour force should suffer through an error of judgement on the part of management. But wherever the management came from, such an error of judgement as regards the market would have been equally possible. To preserve the symmetry one would expect workers to benefit from brilliance on the part of management.

Profit and risk

The trouble with regarding profit as the reward for risk is that both are open-ended. How much profit for how much risk? Does any degree of risk justify any degree of profit? This is the primary social objection to profit as a concept. Excess profit is seen as theft. Risk is forgotten about and in any case must have been the outcome of bad judgement. The added value concept of profits, supported in the UK by Dr Frank Jones, seems to be a better communicating word. Added value is what you get when you subtract the price of goods and services bought in from the receipts on sales. That is the value that the organisation has added to the raw ingredients. Although the breakdown varies from industry to industry, depending for example on the labour content, Dr Jones gives the following figures as a comparison between Japan and the UK. Employees take 52 per cent of added value in the UK and 42 per cent in Japan. The government, through taxes, takes 35 per cent in the UK and only 18.5 per cent in Japan. The investors take only 4 per cent in the UK and as much as 22 per cent in Japan. This last figure may be misleading because Japanese industry runs largely on borrowed money rather than equity capital. In the UK only 9 per cent is available for re-investment whilst in Japan no less than 18.5 per cent is ploughed back into plant. I prefer the term 'work value' (wv) to added value because it indicates directly the value of the work done on the ingredients.

We can imagine a corporation that was owned by no one. For start-up funds there would be risk bonds which we might call 'angel bonds' by analogy with the backers of theatrical ventures. These bonds would be bought by investors and guaranteed by the government. There would be a ceiling of double or treble their purchase price on the bonds, so when the company had prospered enough it could buy back the bonds. Alternatively other investors could loan the company money to buy back its own angel bonds. From then on the corporation would be financed entirely by loans with an interest rate that was calculated as a fixed fraction of the total added value. This would fluctuate with the success of the company so creating a secondary market, not unlike the stock market. Investors could make a capital profit on their bonds but no investors would own the company. No one would. It would be managed by effective managers like any other company. The managers would be appointed partly by the work force and partly by an executive board originally set up by the founders (but not owners) of the enterprise.

In terms of the profit concept we could consider some alternatives. For example, instead of profit being related to the capital employed (as a reward for risk and an incentive for investment) it could be related to the human capital of the people employed. We could imagine a new type of industrial animal in which the management or investors were allowed a certain amount of profit per head of each employee. This could be done as a percentage of the total wage bill. Thus the onus would be on management to employ as many people as possible in order to increase profits. Naturally management would have to employ the people productively otherwise there would be no added value from which to draw the profits (there would be no government subsidy). This might be attractive in times of unemployment and it might anyway be an effective concept in the service industry. Management would be encouraged to expand its work force but also to equip each worker with the capital support that ensured he earned his profit for the company.

The trinity system

We could perhaps develop a totally new concept for industry by 'unbundling' its components. There would be three parts that together went to make up the trinity. Labour would be supplied by a specific 'people-employing-company' which would contract labour to the organisation. That company would be responsible for looking after the labour, recruiting it, paying it and dealing with redundancies and labour relations problems. This would be a natural role for the unions when they are ready to take a more positive part in the economy. It could also be a role for the organisation 'nodes' mentioned at different places in the book.

The second element of the 'trinity' would be the buildings and machinery which would be owned by investors (possibly special 'banks') and rented to the corporation. The third element would be a management team with a management contract. Each of the three elements would be entitled to a fixed share of the added value. For example if labour became more efficient then the same sum of money would be shared out amongst fewer people. It might also be agreed that the owners of the plant would have to re-invest in new plant a fixed proportion of the added value at the discretion of the managers and work-force. If not, the management could rent further plant from other sources. So the three elements of labour, management and capital would contribute to the over-all trinity in a pre-set working arrangement that was to the benefit of all.

In such a system wages would be determined by the people-employing-company as a lump contract sum. Industrial disputes would be handled within that people-employing-company (PEC). Workers could choose to which PEC they wanted to belong just as they choose today whether to join one contractor or another.

Industrial democracy

With the managerial concept of industry as distinct from the capitalist concept the problem of industrial democracy is not so acute. Decisions are made for the sake of the effective running of the company, not for the capital appreciation of the stockholders. In this sense the work-force will naturally be represented both in choice of management and also in management decisions. But, we may hope, this involvement would be positive rather than an 'us against them'. There would be no 'them' because managers are just as much part of the work-force as the workers.

The total wages bill would be set as a fixed portion of the added value so workers would be in favour of new technology that increased the added value without increasing the work force. Redundancies would be handled by payments, re-training schemes, transition subsidies and a coherent positive social policy towards employment.

Capital investment

The reluctance of investors to invest in times of uncertainty is one of the key weaknesses of the market economy and as such will be considered later. Another weakness is the preference for investing in building when building is booming and in land in times of inflation. Investors may also find that they make more profit by dealing with money, as with loans to governments, than by investing in manufacturing. The days of the stock-market booms are possibly over because institutional investors are much less greedy than private investors. For example many investors in the USA are content to put their funds into 'index funds', which simply reflect the Dow Jones index and rise and fall with it – so removing the speculative element of chasing one stock after another. If the market rises a greedy private investor might hang on for future gains. A money manager will tend to sell out and take his profit because at the end of the year he will have to show 'performance'.

Japanese industry (also to some extent German industry) has benefited from a very high rate of personal saving brought about by the lack of welfare and insurance services in Japan. Saving is encouraged by the government who in fact allow the interest on the first six million yen of savings to be tax-free (contrast this with the income tax surcharge of 15 per cent levied on unearned income in the UK to accord with socialist principles). In 1974 the savings ratio in Japan was 24.6 per cent. In Germany it was 15.8 per cent and in the UK it was 9.8 per cent. 79.6 per cent of the saving Japanese said they were saving for illness or a 'rainy day', and 54.2 per cent also mentioned they were saving for weddings (which are extraordinarily expensive in Japan) and the children's education. The saved money is then lent by banks to industry. In contrast in the UK the saved money is put into building societies and lent-out for housing or lent to the government for welfare spending. To be fair the uncertainty of the business climate in the UK with price restraints, inflation and wage demands makes industry reluctant to invest in any case.

If we wanted to encourage consumption in order to reflate the economy then we might try to alter the conceptual difference between spending and saving. At the moment a family might have the choice between spending money on a new car and keeping it in the building society in case of emergency or unemployment. In times of recession or uncertainty the savings rise but of course they are useless because industry will not invest. So the Keynesian pump-priming never gets going. If consumers could be persuaded that their money was as safe in a car as in a building society they might spend more. This would involve a guaranteed buy-back scheme so that if the money was required the car could be sold back to a central body on a guaranteed price basis. It would then be sold off in the second-hand market. In effect it would be a sort of insurance and it could be worked out on an insurance basis. Naturally the owner would expect to pay for the use of the car whilst it was in his possession. What would be valuable to him, would be that the money would still be usable as money (most of it) in case of emergency or the 'rainy day' that 79.6 per cent of the Japanese savers said they had in mind.

The encouragement of investment in times of reluctance requires new concepts of reward for risk-taking. We might even consider a negative interest-rate – that is to say a company or entrepreneur would actually be paid for trying to use capital productively.

Summary

In most countries there has been a quiet evolution from the capitalist economy to the managerial economy. With exceptions, the major sources of capital are in institutional hands. This managerial economy allows us to develop new concepts of industry. Some concepts mentioned here include the trinity system, the PEC (people-employing-company), the corporation that no one owns, the concept of profit per head, and the distribution of added value on a fixed share basis. The decision ownership of capital can be separated from the value ownership and that is the basis of the managerial economy. Here we might also introduce the concept of 'usufruct' which allows complete ownership with the single exception of sale. We might also, in the future, introduce the concept of retrospective sales to discourage speculation and increase the movement of assets. For example a young Spaniard in Majorca was so poor that he could not afford the £80 needed to fence in 50,000 square yards of land he had inherited. So he sold the lot for £25. A few years later the tourist boom arrived and that same plot was sold for £10 million. With the concept of retrospective sales a seller would be entitled to benefit from the immediately following re-sale through receiving a fixed amount of the added value (for example 25 per cent). This might encourage people to sell assets they could not use productively themselves.

There is much scope for changing some of our archaic concepts of industry and production. Now that we are moving out of the industrial age into the age of organisation we can devise new instruments and new industrial animals that encourage productivity. We need to handle risk and reward on a much more sophisticated basis. We can certainly reduce risk in many cases and we can be more positive about reward. It is unlikely that we shall be able to regulate industry into productivity but we can work to remove uncertainty and to create structures that encourage positive effort rather than a defence of poor performance.

14 THE ECONOMY AND TRADE

There was a time when religion occupied the minds of men. The next preoccupation was military power-plays and battles and empires. Today economics are the central theme. What is perhaps surprising is how poorly developed are our concepts of economics. We can treat economics as a mathematical exercise but we soon run into an enormous amount of trouble as we try to quantify the effect of one variable on another. Just how does the availability of money push up prices – is it perhaps the unavailability of lack-of-money that does that? Econometric models are most useful and the computer will be a great help here because it will allow us to improve our models and to try in a few seconds an economic theory that might have taken several generations to try in real life.

Instead of the mathematical approach we could take the historical approach but the trouble is that economic reality is moving much too fast. Lessons from the past may be quite inapplicable to the present. For example the sheer speed of technology allows decisions to be made almost simultaneously all over the world and the action (for instance shifting currencies) to be effected immediately. Keynesian remedies might have applied in the nineteen-thirties but may not today. Pump-priming in a service economy may not produce the same effect – furthermore an increase in consumption need not feed through to an increase in manufacturing because imports are sucked in (as indeed happened in the consumer boom in the UK in the summer of 1978).

The problem is that economics are much more intimately connected with psychology than anyone likes to admit. The psychology of investment is the psychology of confidence. The psychology of value may be one of hope or of panic. Consumer behaviour (spending or saving) is characteristically unpredictable except as regards the mini-booms that follow obvious hold-backs. The effect of incentives and regulations on behaviour is another area of importance. Nor is it all common sense. Logic-bubbles do work very well in economics but assessing individual perceptions at any moment is not easy. We need much focused thinking in this area and several chairs of economic psychology.

The market economy

This is the traditional free-enterprise system. It is based on people's free choice as to what they want to buy, the price they want to buy at and what they want to invest their money in. In a sense it is economic democracy and is therefore attractive. Artificial attempts to create value usually end in failure. Market economy theories are based on two sorts of value: the first is value-value and the second is use-value. Use-value is the true value when something is in use, like the value of a motor-car for getting you from place to place. Value-value is based on psychology. If I have what you want then you are prepared to pay the price that matches your want – but does not necessarily match the use you are going to get out of it. An art dealer is delighted to buy a Rembrandt at the highest possible price he can. The high price will put up the value of all other Rembrandts and his profit will be higher on a high price (as a proportion) than on a low price.

He knows he can sell on at a profit because there are so few Rembrandts on the market. The museum want to buy at a low price so that for the same budget they can buy more pictures for their public. The museum does not want to sell on but to fill a gap in its art collection. The dealer is using value-value and the museum is using use-value. It is the problem between the two sorts of value that creates all the abuse and injustices of a market economy. Obviously any monopoly or near monopoly situation – whether in manufacturing or in labour supply – allows value-value to dominate use-value to the point of extortion.

The health service in the UK is very short of anaesthetists because over two-thirds of those trained in the UK leave for better posts abroad. One anaesthetist was earning £6,000 per annum in the UK and on moving to Germany his pay increased to more than £20,000 a year. Had he gone to the USA he might soon have been earning over £50,000. The anaesthetist can use the free choice of a market economy. But could the UK afford to pay him USA prices in order to keep him? Even if he repaid the cost of his UK education he would still have occupied a training post that did not yield a productive value to the UK. There have been several failures in well-established travel companies in the USA following the introduction of low air-fares by scheduled airlines. That seems reasonable because if the companies no longer offered the consumer an advantage they had no value. But the scheduled lines could decide to drop their low fares at any time and the travel companies could not be built up overnight. Farmers buy a lot of hens. They start laying and 200 million eggs a week are produced in the UK – there is a glut and prices fall. Shipping owners all decide that the market conditions are right for building tankers so they all build tankers and there is a glut and in 1977 the value of tanker tonnage fell by up to 50 per cent. In 1972 the top fifteen US banks had 72.7 per cent of their funds committed to industrial stocks. By 1977 this had fallen to 54.1 per cent.

The strengths of the market economy are also its weaknesses. If something is a good thing then everyone decides to do it at once and there is a property boom followed by a collapse. As property prices rise so investors anticipate further rises and buy in order to sell on at a profit. They borrow money from the bank and pay the interest out of the profitable sales of the properties whilst the boom lasts. Then it runs out of steam. Some properties have to be sold at a slight loss in order to pay bank interest charges due. This causes a panic and everyone tries to get out of property at once. The market collapses and properties fall to a fraction of their 'true' value. In this example we have most of the faults of the market economy: stampede, anticipation of value rises, self-fulfilling prophecy, rise in prices due to scarcity, glut and collapse, boom and bust fluctuations.

The intention of the market economy is that value-value should be used in order to produce use-value. In other words you buy a company that makes shoes in order to make shoes. But if value-value pursues value-value then there is a positive feed-back and wild fluctuations in price with speculation and no real use produced for anyone. There is the famous story of the man who bought some sardines from a black-marketeer during the Second World War. On opening the tins he found the sardines inedible, so he complained. The seller expressed astonishment that the buyer should have opened the tins: 'those tins are not for eating,' he said, 'they are just for buying and selling'.

The self-fulfilling prophecy means that if everyone holds back awaiting a devaluation this may be forced in order to get the economy moving again. If all the buyers of government bonds hold back awaiting a change in interest rates then this also may be forced. If investors lose confidence in the stockmarket and sell, then the market falls and the loss of confidence seems justified. The market economy is based on confidence and anticipation. In times of uncertainty investment falls when it is most needed. Just how powerful this confidence effect may be is shown by the construction of a skyscraper on New York's Fifth Avenue. The second largest and most sophisticated bank in the USA was prepared to walk away from a mortgage of about $45 million because they did not feel that rental rates (following a period of overbuilding) would rise to $12 a square foot. The construction company also had to walk away from its investment and a $100 million building was eventually sold for $35 million. About two years later rents were up to $18 a square foot.

The opposite of a market economy is a regulated and planned economy. This has as many defects and perhaps more. Order is produced by regulation and restraint and artificial controls which never work well because by the time they are seen to be necessary it is too late for them to act in time, and by the time (when they have worked through) they do act they may be more harmful than useful. Investments are made not on the grounds of need or true use-value but for political purposes and hence productive value cannot be spurred by market pull. There is little or no positive input except incentives that are either too small to work or large enough to attract inefficient producers anyway. Failure is cushioned or subsidised thus providing unfair competition for others and removing the natural competitive incentive.

We badly need new economic concepts based on the reality of a complex world that cannot afford the wild fluctuations of speculation or the stagnation of defensive regulation. Perhaps we ought to look at the tandem concept that is used from time to time: you are free to do something – provided you do something else as well. In other words you are free to invest in one direction provided that at the same time you also invest in another, designated, direction. You are free to build speculative office buildings provided you also build low cost housing at the same time. So the ebullience of the market system can be retained but speculation restrained and real value produced. To have a machine with no energy is pointless, to have one that is full of energy but races away for its own benefit is also pointless: we need an energetic machine that is also harnessed usefully. Too often we assume that just to slow down the machine, by braking it, is to harness it.

Trade

The UK car worker is said to produce only half as much as the German car worker even when both have the same equipment. If the price, design and quality are better then a consumer may prefer a Japanese car to a UK one. This is exporting employment and importing unemployment. The cry is for tariff protection. Korea with its Hyundai plant is about to become a major car exporter. The technology is easy to acquire and a new plant is probably more modern than existing plant elsewhere. As for design, you just pay an Italian designer in the same way as Volkswagen might. Included in the price of the British car is the cost of safety regulations at work, welfare, workers' pensions and so on. But this may not be the case with imported cars. Whether it is such hidden costs, or production efficiency, or the lower living standards of overseas workers, the final outcome is a 'better value' car available for the consumer. Tariff protection protects the home worker by asking the consumer to subsidise his work habits and management style. It is argued that tariff protection is self-defeating in the long run because it reduces the ability of other countries to buy exports from the home country and so ultimately reduces jobs.

Some countries, like Japan, have been very clever – by design or intention– in operating 'procedural' tariffs. That is to say there are no official tariffs on imports but the distribution channel is so complicated that the price of the import in the shops is much higher than that of the locally produced goods. Then there are procedural tariffs such as emission regulations for cars which the government can agree with local producers ahead of time. So in effect there are tariff barriers. Japan sells more to the Common Market and the USA than she imports from them (a current account surplus) but on the other hand she runs a deficit with Australia, the Middle East and Latin America because Japan has to import almost all its raw materials and fuel. So Japan really exports added value and the country seems good at adding value.

Quotas are a form of protection. A shoe store in Vancouver has to get special permission from Ottawa to import ten pairs of shoes for a customer because the imports have to fall within the quota – otherwise low cost producers like Brazil and Korea will swamp the market and kill local industry.

We might eventually have to develop two sorts of currency: for example the ordinary pound and the export pound. The export pound would be earned by exporters. Importers would have to buy these export pounds from the central bank in order to pay for imports. There would be a free market as to the premium paid for the export pounds and this would feed back to the exporters who earned them. Overall trade balance would then be self-adjusting. Exporting would become more profitable and only the best value imports would survive. In essence the scheme would have similarities with the dollar premium operating in the UK for those who want to invest capital abroad.

Currencies

We may come to change our concepts of currency. On the international level there will probably be a creation of a more fluid form of the SDR (Special Drawing Rights) to create a currency not linked to the US need to import oil. In Europe the Common Market may well create its own common currency.

The Swiss will probably have to create a mini-franc for internal use if they are not to be priced out of the international market through the appreciation of their currency. What is required is a use-value currency which is not linked to the economic performance of one country and not subject to the value-value speculation associated with gold (which also has a limited, politically vulnerable supply and an industrial usage). There are those who believe that devices of this sort do not really do more than a free market does anyway. There are others who believe that by simplifying thinking they can lead to whole new strategies and concepts.

We should not forget the $400 billion of Eurodollars which are outside the control of any government and are administered by banks internationally.

Within a country we may come to use alternative currencies. For example one currency may be targeted and have a higher value when used for food than for other things. This would be an elaboration of the food-stamp concept. As soon as there is more than one currency then targeting becomes possible. It might also be possible to stabilise one currency with regard to a basket of purchases so giving, in effect, an internal gold standard not subject to international speculation as with gold. A basic part of every wage might be paid in this super-currency. Of course one would have to be very careful as to how alternative currencies were fed into the economy or removed from it, otherwise the bad currency would simply drive out the good one according to the classic Gresham's Law. Speculation and anticipated value changes would also have to be kept in mind. But the concept of plural currencies gives a powerful tool both for regulation and for psychological reality (for example in making visible the effect of inflation on one currency but not on another which has been indexed).

Inflation

Until thrown somewhat off course by the hike in oil prices, Brazil coped satisfactorily with inflation by indexing everything in sight. The Swiss index wages and rents. Astonishingly rents are actually reduced if there is negative inflation (as can happen in Switzerland on account of the currency appreciation). Elsewhere the ratchet effect means that inflation, like expectations, only ratchets upwards.

The monetarist approach to inflation is a tight control on the money supply. Imagine a 'timid currency' that actually withdrew from the economy at the first hint of inflation. Such a currency would not earn interest when deposited in an account – on the other hand it would be indexed so that its value would keep pace with inflation. Normally there would be no point in holding such a currency since it would be at a disadvantage when related to ordinary interest-earning currency. But in times of inflation a point is reached when indexing preserves value better than interest (especially after-tax interest). So ordinary currency would be converted into the 'timid currency' which would withdraw from the market. Furthermore the deposited timid currency could not be used by banks as a basis for lending. In many ways the timid currency would act like gold except that it would be local in its use, not subject to supply problems and not subject to value-value speculations. The gold price can be forced up by the pressure of buying against speculative reluctance to sell. Speculation of this sort would be impossible with the timid currency because supply would not be limited. The timid currency, which could also be called 'local gold', would be a sort of stage in the life of ordinary money – a sort of dormant stage. What effect would the timid currency have on industrial investment and productivity? This would be a matter for regulation. Once money has been inactivated in this way it can be reactivated for special purposes – for example by allowing interest on the timid currency for certain investment purposes.

The Third World

I have not dealt much with the Third World in this book because I feel that a positive future in the developed countries would be the first prerequisite for better prospects all round. Whilst the developed countries are in a negative mood they are less likely to consider the positive cooperation that the Third World needs. I feel that the Third World must develop its own concepts and life-styles rather than ape concepts which are already becoming outmoded in the developed countries. I see no reason why Third World countries have to follow the different stages of the 'concept-adolescence' of the developed countries. I would like to see them develop their own philosophies and organisational styles. The high technology they can borrow directly for that is universal.

The priorities of the Third World must be: deliberate creation of an effective organisational class (which is not the same as a middle class); development of an appropriate educational system and content (not a copy of the cumbersome and wasteful system in use in developed countries); development of a managerial style of government (not dialectical power politics); design of specific concepts for industrial and agricultural development; design of concepts for stable trading with the rest of the world; decisions and action on birth control.

The rest of the world can help by means of orderly commodity markets; credit and loan financing for projects; aid for self-help operations; the cooperative creation of institutions that will help with the priorities listed in the previous paragraph. The benevolent but patronising missionary attitude should be replaced by managerial concepts. The Third World should not see itself as a third class developed world, but as a first class developing world with its own road to choose.

Summary

Our economic thinking is in something of a mess because events have outstripped our ability to handle them – or even learn from them. We are too busy coping with what is urgent to think about what is important. We try to ride highly unstable systems and when we try to control them we usually succeed in killing them. The twin objectives of economic growth and political expediency cannot both be achieved but we do not have the means or the courage to say so. We are forced to prefer economics by crisis management because we cannot be convinced that any theory will work, or that any structure can be designed to anticipate the requirements of the future. We can accept restrictive theories, or theories that have at least the justification of political attractiveness, but we are wary, perhaps rightly, of positive theories because they might turn out to be dangerous. In a fog of uncertainty it makes sense to drive slowly – but it also helps to clean the windscreen. That is the purpose of thinking that is positive rather than defensive.

15 POLITICS AND GOVERNMENT

Democracy is a pretty poor system – but, as so many people have pointed out, the others are a good deal worse. Could technology not provide us with an all-wise benevolent dictator with a remote-controlled bomb inserted in his abdomen? If enough people telephoned the right number simultaneously then this expression of dissatisfaction would cause the bomb to explode and disintegrate the dictator. The bomb would be placed around his aorta so that his first task on election could not be to order a surgeon to remove it.

The advantages of democracy are all negative and many of them arise directly from the CYA attitude. It is an incredible concept when you consider that it can serve to keep quiet more than half the population for many years whilst the other half governs them. When the Labour party are in power in the UK it could be said that government is in accordance with the 28 per cent of the electorate who belong to trade unions – and even then many of these are Tories. But the election losers keep more or less quiet because they have had a chance and will have a chance again next time round. If, of course, they are in a permanent minority like the Catholics in Northern Ireland then the minority is forever denied a say in government. What is even more extraordinary is that in fact the election of a government is probably decided by a 3 per cent, some of whom may not care much about politics anyway. If the party faithfuls stick to their party line then the election is decided by the swinging voters who flick from one side to the other according to boredom, personality and whim.

Electing a representative does not really matter too much. We could pick them by a lottery system. What does matter is that once elected the politician's behaviour is strictly governed by what he fears his electors will think about him. This is a continuous exercise of CYA. He has to operate political expediency and dare not do things which are badly required but might be unpopular at first until the positive effect wears through. He has to protect his career and his chosen life style. This is the real exercise of democracy, the election does not matter much. Short term policies must take precedence over long term ones.

A major advantage of democracy is that it prevents a small group of political activists from taking over the country. In many cases in the UK trades unions have been taken over – through the apathy of the members – by a group of activists elected only by their friends who bothered to attend the election meetings. Prevention of such a happening is perhaps the major role of democracy.

Party politics

Democracy is not inseparable from party politics. Party politics happen to be a convenient administrative device for democracy. Parties provide an administrative base and a communicating system with the electors who only have to recognise party slogans instead of personal skill. We can look at some of the general disadvantages of the system. The first is obviously polarisation since each party must pretend that it holds all the wisdom and that everything which the other party does is either wicked or stupid. Similarly it is necessary to attack everything and to create for yourself an apparently different policy – even if you know the other policy to be correct. Policies have to be immediately popular and protected from attack since the opposition will welcome any opportunity to attack.

As far as possible it is best to have a policy of doing nothing because most politicians suspect that electors vote against the other party's mistakes rather than in favour of virtues. So if you make no mistakes you are safe. And if you do nothing you are not going to make any mistakes. A party is stuck with the sacred cows and doctrines that have been useful in the past but are now just an encumbrance.

The electorate has to accept a total package of policies. There is no unbundling even if one policy from one party makes sense but another policy from the other party is better than that of one's own party. There is no picking and choosing. Except on rare occasions the politician has to vote the party line.

In practice party politics are going to get more and more difficult if not impossible. This is because there has to be converging conservatism for a number of reasons. The costs of on-growing programmes are large and there is relatively little of the budget that can be played around with. Change is expensive and so are new projects. Any definite policy may upset some section and provide the mistake that is going to hang around the neck of the party at the election. Most issues are so complex that there is only one source of expert opinion so both parties have to follow the same course (like the acceptance of monetarism in times of inflation). The cosmetic politics of gesture becomes possible and so real action is unnecessary. If you always say the right thing and show that your heart is in the right place you do not actually have to do anything.

The media

The technology of the media has had a profound effect on the realities of politics. If I had to list the major power bases in modern day society I would list: the media, the unions, the institutional investors, protest groups (acting through the media) and government employees (in the USA, government employees make up 16.5 per cent of the electorate).

The media, and especially television, put a great premium on appearance and personality. If a man looks avuncular, as does Jim Callaghan, then he is regarded as such. If a person looks shifty he is regarded as such. All this may have nothing whatsoever to do with the candidate's true personality let alone his governing ability. The media put a premium on skill in winning the election. But skill in winning an election may have nothing to do with skill in government.

The media create a terror of investigation or exposure and undoubtedly this is a very positive point for the media. Ralph Nader could not have operated without the media. In the UK programmes like 'That's Life' with Esther Rantzen keep bureaucracy on its toes. Investigating journalism pioneered by the *Sunday Times*' 'Insight' concept exposes major scandals like the alleged BP and Shell supply of oil to Rhodesia in spite of the sanctions. Today the cry of politicians everywhere is 'get those people off my back'. The Vietnam War was brought to an end by media pressure as was Richard Nixon. The power is for the good, but it is enormous and it is unelected in any way and also unaccountable. In the final analysis it is worth having because it does keep politicians honest and on their toes, but it may also serve to foster the CYA attitude of never daring to do anything.

The media create a powerful means for persuasion. It may be that choosing an effective advertising agent will seriously alter your party's chances in the election. When does the sheer efficiency of persuasion become manipulation?

The media create news or rather respond willy-nilly to media-type stories. Any protest group such as the National Front in the UK can more or less compel the media to give it attention, as can any hi-jacker or kidnapper, by doing something the media cannot resist. The Grunwick dispute was a major issue whilst the scenes of policemen restraining picket lines were shown daily on TV. Then it disappeared from the screen – mainly through boredom – and the issue just died completely.

The media also make possible totally new techniques of democracy by allowing people to express an opinion on an issue. The statistics of polls have been worked out pretty reliably and within a certain margin of error (not more than 5 per cent) it is possible by sampling a few thousand people to have a view that is likely to represent the feeling of the entire nation on an issue. The polls are published in the papers and people can then react to them either way – by joining the bandwagon or by being contrary. It will not be long before it becomes possible via an ordinary television set to indicate your views on a particular matter. For example a politician presenting an issue on television could get an immediate feedback on what the viewers felt. In America in a trial area there is already the QUBE system which uses cable television and allows this direct feedback in a very sophisticated way (for example the response from different parts of the town or country can be separately identified, even that from an individual house).

The media make possible cosmetic politics or the politics of gesture. I was once on the Kupcinet television show in Chicago with a well-known political figure. I happened to disagree with some points he made. He immediately said, 'Yes, I agree with that point,', which left me with nothing to say since it would have been difficult to go back and show why he should not have been agreeing with me. A skilled politician knows how to handle questions and issues and how always to make the right gestures. If a statement turns out to be unpopular it can then be claimed that it was 'Misinterpreted'.

Representatives and leaders

No one is quite sure whether an elected politician is supposed to represent his electors or to lead them. If we were to look at possible layers of activity in government we might find five layers.

There was a time when a politician himself might also be an expert in economics or agriculture or war. That has long since ceased to be the case. So the first layer of wisdom is that of the expert and this is tapped in Senate Committees in the USA, reports, Royal Commissions or through expert institutes like the Brookings Institute.

The second layer is that of the creative or constructive leadership which is supposed to create policies and initiatives. Whether it does so or not depends on the political climate and the talent of the people who are supposed to do it. A leader needs a sensitivity to public opinion but this talent by itself is not enough: a mirror is never going to be a searchlight.

Then we come to the main political layer: a body of people who are supposed to represent the people of the country. Straight representation would, presumably, not be enough, else we could simply select a chamber by a lottery system much as we select a jury for a court – with the emphasis on the ordinary man. The elected representative is supposed to be very much wiser. He is supposed to understand the complex economic issues and to interpret them for his constituents and even to decide how the issues will affect his constituents. There is always a divided loyalty because he must represent both his own home town area, which may require more defence spending to keep its employment up, and the country which may require less defence spending in order to reduce government spending and taxation.

The fourth layer is the ordinary person for whom the whole machinery has been set up so that he can approve or otherwise of the policies that are being presented. The whole third layer is only there because the ordinary person does not have the time, inclination or intelligence to become involved – so he delegates his interest. But today we could create a sort of 'jury chamber'. When a person voted at an election he would also draw a lottery ticket at the same time. In this way a random selection of people would be appointed to the jury chamber. Before this non-party chamber the politicians would present their cases much as a lawyer does in court. The jury would give their verdict. After all the verdict of your fellow party-members in the political chamber is pretty useless except in coalition politics. The jury could be changed each month. Or it could stay at home and operate through special television/telephone links.

The fifth layer is that of administration which is involved with keeping things running, getting things done and carrying out the decisions of the political layer. Switzerland operates remarkably well under a government of administration. Few people know the names of Swiss politicians. It is enough that they get on with the job of maintaining the framework of the country and making sure that the trains run on time and the Swiss franc remains sound. Hong Kong operates a similar system, for the four million Chinese are content to let a few thousand colonial Englishmen run an efficient (and very efficient it is) framework within which they can get on with the serious business of family and making money. The growth rate is 9 per cent a year. The Swiss have referendums from time to time on such things as whether foreigners should be asked to leave or whether there should be a subway system in Zürich. The system is not easily applied to all economic decisions.

It may be that the direction of evolution of politics will be towards a managerial system run by levels one, two and five with the retention of level three for the sake of the media and cosmetic politics. Managers have usually made poor politicians because management is the art of the necessary whereas politics is the art of the possible.

Class-based two-party politics is probably an anachronism but until it dies there might be a case (for instance in the UK) for a bi-party committee which would consider fundamental policies on a nonparty basis. There are many matters where the effectiveness of the policy is of more importance than the scoring of political points. The American committee system seems to make more sense in this respect. The aim should be to get the energy and skill of politicians directed towards more productive ends than scoring debating points. To prove that you are right by showing the other fellow to be a fool seems to leave in abeyance the question of whether both parties might be wrong. It is fortunate for politicians that in general they seem to be held in low regard by the public for that way not much is expected of them.

Proportional representation tends to create weak government but gives a chance for individual parties to bargain on different issues and is therefore more fair to minority groups. Voting on specific propositions at the time of elections, on the American model, would also seem to make sense. The technology that will shortly be available in TV will make frequent shopping-list referendums quite feasible and there will be a danger in the over-simplifying of issues and a lack of constructive leadership.

Ideally one would like to see the creation of alternative systems of government within one country. People could then choose, in a practical manner, which system suited them best – voting with their feet rather than with their opinion. The creation of the organisation 'nodes' discussed earlier, as separate feudal states of organisation, could open up interesting possibilities. There would be lump sum dealings with such nodes and the community style administration of the node would then make its own distribution decisions. It would be a sort of local government but not on a geographical basis.

Government and tax

The famous Proposition 13 that was passed in California in spite of the opposition of the governor, Jerry Brown, may prove to be as significant in American politics as the Boston Tea-party. Both protests were over taxation and on the face of it the California tax situation seems to be as immoral. Property taxes are levied on the current asset value of a property. The sudden boom in real estate prices in California (created by a mixture of speculation, protection against inflation, and the inclination of too many people to move to California) meant that for an individual who had lived quietly in his house the property tax might suddenly double or treble. If you bought a house for $30,000 and then one day someone in your row sold his house for $60,000 then your property tax would double. If you could not afford it you had to move out. The effect is, of course, equivalent to a government deciding to double or treble taxes and no government would dare to do that directly. In general the effect is similar in its immorality to the failure of the UK government to index tax bands as has been done in Australia.

So there was a powerful cause for the passage of Proposition 13 but once passed the proposition has a much wider significance – as did the Boston Tea-party – for it serves to indicate to government that the days of high taxes and big government spending are limited. The immediate effect of Proposition 13 is said to be a cutting of 86,000 jobs in the public sector. A backlash is expected because government employees are already a significant voting sector of the electorate (16.5 per cent of the work force in the US as a whole). One cannot really conceive the development of a 'government party' determined to keep up the 'big government' policy, but government is now such a large employer that the idea is horrifying.

One hundred years ago the tax collected by the government in the UK was £33 million, today it is £21,000 million. Some of that is due to inflation and population increase but the part that is not shows the increase in the size of government involvement. There is no reason why everyone should not ultimately work for the government except that this experiment in communist countries does not seem to have increased the quality of life or the productive wealth. The other alternative would be to devolve many of the functions of government on to separate organisations like the suggested 'nodes'. It is claimed that in New York City private refuse collection systems are eight times as efficient as the public ones. In the United States many groups of people are now hiring private policemen to patrol their streets. Another way to cut government expenditure would be to make use of the NML (non-market-labour) scheme suggested earlier. For example the beautification of a place of work might be the responsibility of those working there: they could provide the materials and the NML would provide the labour. To keep a close eye on government wastage an independent inspectorate could be established with the power to set up focused inquiries.

The proportion of revenue provided by indirect tax (VAT) is 10 per cent in the UK, 20 per cent in France and 15 per cent in Germany. There is much to be said for reducing income tax so that a worker receives more money in his pocket, and then letting him decide how he wants to spend it. The problem of such a change-over (which would cause immediate price rises) is a nice example of the edge effect and also of the sort of change which politicians would find very hard. There would be a danger of triggering an inflationary spiral with wage demands pushing up underlying prices. Perhaps a straight 10 per cent increase in take-home pay would be announced simultaneously with the 10 per cent increase in prices.

Summary

Short of a revolution there seems no way for a political system to evolve, for the vested interests of those running it and the legitimate fears of those supporting it must regard any suggested change as dangerous experiment. As a system democracy has a lot of advantages and most of them are negative – this is not to say they are not invaluable, after all the value of a poison label on a poison bottle is negative in that it prevents you doing something. It seems a pity that much of the operation of party politics is concerned with churning the air and scoring debating points. Perhaps in the future the cosmetic value of party politics will be recognised as such and the managerial aspects will quietly proceed with running the government. The media have made a big difference to politics in terms of exposure and the personality cult. Politicians have to behave better than ever before but their behaviour may be directed solely at avoiding mistakes and hence initiatives. The jury system of direct appeal through polls, referendums or TV feedback or even a jury chamber will undoubtedly increase in the future and might succeed in shifting political decisions from personalities or party doctrines to issues.

Government expenditure and growth are likely to be restricted by an overt or covert tax strike. There may be a devolution of some government functions to other organised bodies like the suggested 'nodes'. At the same time people involvement in government services on a 'social contribution' basis could be encouraged.

16 LAW AND ORDER

For most people the most important quality of life that is expected from society is law and order. This would come ahead of health, education, employment, wages and anything else. For the sake of law and order citizens are prepared to give up democracy.

It is possible to take the 'tax' view of crime. That is to say that a certain amount of crime is a necessary tax on life. If we want to use cars then we must accept a sort of tax of 7,000 road deaths a year in the UK. If we want to smoke cigarettes we accept the tax of 38,000 cancer deaths a year. Some people will be struck by lightning. Some people will fall off cliffs. There will always be some psychotics. So if we value freedom and live in a complex society we must accept a certain measure of crime as a tax on life. If you visit New York and are mugged you should regard that $200 you lose as a sort of visitor's tax. The argument is that attempts to stamp out crime lead quickly to a police state and are ineffective anyway. If we look at the actual crime figures we might accept this point of view. There were 746 homicides in New York in 1967 and in 1977 the figure had doubled to 1,552, but was still small relative to the population. But the one fatal flaw in this argument is that of fear. When you smoke a cigarette or drive carelessly you always assume that the tragedy is going to happen to someone else. With crime you fear it is going to happen to you and, unlike the other situations, there is little you can do to prevent it. If an old lady walks down the same dark street every night of her life but is in fact never mugged she still suffers the fear of mugging 365 days a year. That is why crime so easily destroys the quality of life. That is why it must make sense for law and order to be the top priority in any civilisation.

Sin and crime

Much of our thinking about crime is based on the medieval notion of sin. The criminal is a sinner and must be punished. Moreover the punishment must be proportional to the sin. The criminal will be deterred from crime, just as he is deterred from sin by visions of hell-fire. I think we need to forget about this concept of sin and consider instead a concept of social pollution. Pollution detracts from the quality of life and needs removing. There may be no more feeling of resentment towards a criminal than towards a mad person but society is not able to tolerate destructive behaviour of that sort. On this basis a mindless vandal may be judged to be more anti-social in his behaviour than a provoked murderer. A person who for no reason sets out to wreck an aspect of society is a serious pollutant.

The severity of the deterrent is much less important than the strong likelihood of getting caught and the likelihood of being swiftly sentenced. Punishment need not be harsh in terms of being crude but the sentenced person should have to genuinely work his way back into society by earning money to pay off his debt. A sentence could be in 'earnings' terms not in 'time' terms. A disciplined environment, possibly under military supervision, in which the work was to take place would constitute the prison. It is not punishment but the unfitness of a person for society that matters.

The average daily prison population in the UK is 27,876. What is extraordinary is that 50 per cent of those released will offend again within a year. This suggests that once they have crossed the threshold to being a criminal they identify and behave as one. The usual threshold inhibitions no longer apply. It may be that they have no other way of earning a living once they get outside but this seems much less likely, for other people on welfare payments do not resort to crime. It may be that a criminal is institutionalised and in some way regards prison as his base. If provision of a reasonable pension kept a prisoner out of prison that would be worthwhile.

The concept of criminality as social pollution carries with it a ruthlessness that is not present when we consider crime as sin. With sin we might look for the extenuating circumstances and the deprived background but with pollution we look at the fact not the reason behind it. The schooling of a difficult horse is the schooling of a difficult horse not the exploration of his behaviour – unless the exploration helps the schooling.

Types of crime

One judge told another that he would do well in court if he just remembered the ten commandments and added a further one for motoring offences. We can create crime by creating laws. The corruption in the Hong Kong police force was caused by the existence of Victorian laws on gambling. Laws on prostitution should sensibly be directed not at the fact but at exploitation and social pollution. The pragmatic Dutch have a sensible attitude. From time to time the police should be allowed a say in which laws should be dropped and what new ones might be needed. To regard the police as zombies dedicated to the technical operation of the law is to lose an opportunity and to undervalue their role.

In 1976 in the UK there were 1,211,000 motoring offences. Of these 68,000 involved the very serious social offence of drinking and driving (serious because of the danger to others which though unintended is real). Trivial motoring offences create disrespect for the law and the attitude of what-you-can-get-away-with. A reduction in offences through cooperation with motoring organisations and the application of on-the-spot fines would help here.

Another type is the gentle rip-off on the basis that large corporations or bodies won't notice. Last year it was estimated that Londoners stole about £1 million worth of electricity through meter adjustments and fiddles. Tough fines would be the obvious answer since rip-offs have a financial base.

Then come rowdyism, hooliganism and vandalism. The borderline between good-natured high spirits and vandalism is not very clear. In group or gang situations each member is egged on by another. Yet in a social sense this is a serious type of crime because it indicates a lack of social discipline which threatens the quality of life in society. John Harper was kicked to death by four youths who objected to him joining in their singing one evening. Murder was no doubt far from their minds and all they wanted was a bit of 'aggro'. In 1977 of every ten people arrested in London three were between 10 and 16 years old and two between 17 and 20 years old. The figures are reflected in New York where youngsters between 15 and 20 make up only 9 per cent of the population but account for 45 per cent of the violent crime. No doubt it is due to boredom, gang stimulation, the search for kicks, the effects of TV and lack of discipline at home. It may not seem serious but in a way it is the most serious form of crime because of its epidemic nature. Tough discipline in an army training centre might be appropriate – prison would not.

Then there is the mugger (where it is not a teen-age gang looking for kicks), and the burglar for whom criminality is a way of life. Sharply increasing the likelihood of getting caught (decoys for muggers) and the necessity to earn one's way back to civilian life might be required.

The next group might be defined as the more serious professional criminal and would include bank robbery, gangsterism and drug pushing. Although more serious in a 'criminal' sense these types of crime probably have less impact on the general quality of life because they are confined to specific areas.

A whole group of violent criminals including murderers, and those who use excessive violence in any situation, might be considered as psychopaths and – for the protection of society – treated as people who will always have to be separated from society. This would suggest some sort of penal colony which could be quiet and pleasant since punishment would not be the aim. Medical or chemical treatment is another possibility. A rapist may fall into this group or into the mentally ill grouping or into the what-you-can-get-away-with group referred to earlier (vandals, etc.).

As society grows more complex a whole new class of criminal may emerge. He would be exemplified by the computer thief. In the USA the average size of a bank robbery is about $10,000 and the average size of a computer theft is $400,000. Very often computer thefts are never revealed because the loss is covered by insurance and because the financial institution does not wish to publish the breach of security in case the public should lose confidence in it. The interesting point about this type of crime is that it is totally non-violent and does not harm an individual as such (because the loss is spread). On the other hand the amounts may be large. I would suggest that the penalties should be proportional to the total amount of crime of this sort uncovered in one year: the penalties would rise in proportion to the amount of the crime. I would also suggest that the criminal would have to work his way back into society by applying his skills constructively. Recovery of the stolen amounts would also influence the penalty.

The above grouping is not clearcut nor is it comprehensive. The purpose was to show that we may need to develop some clear concept about types of crime which are totally different in nature: the violent criminal is different from the irresponsible vandal; drug pushing is different from computer fraud. They are not simply different degrees of sinfulness as we consider them now.

Suppose there was a suggestion that the penalty for any crime committed on Monday was to be doubled. This would be unthinkable with our traditional concepts of justice and criminality. How could a burglary committed on Monday be twice as bad as one committed on Tuesday? But the suggestion indicates a new attitude to crime. The punishment is not related to the sinfulness of the crime but to society's attitude to that crime. No one *has* to commit a burglary on Monday. If society determines that one type of crime is more dangerous to the quality of life then that may be the criterion. For example mugging may be regarded as more serious than bank robbery because it creates fear in every citizen and forces an alteration in his life style, whereas bank robbers are professionaly concerned with banks that can take precautions.

The police force

It will need to be a priority that the police force is upgraded in status and in pay. Ideally the police force should reach the status of the military in Europe about one hundred years ago. It should almost become an elite profession with the most able people trying to get into it. Pay, training and selection would all need serious consideration. In 1976 the defence budget was £6,176 million and the police budget only £1,137 million. Most citizens would not mind paying more for a better police force provided their extra contribution was earmarked for that purpose.

The fear of detection is probably the best safeguard against crime. For example if it is known that 68 per cent of homicide cases in New York are solved, that must be a powerful deterrent to a cold killing. Television might be used much more extensively to show police successes and to remove from crime the idea that 'you can get away with it'.

The general public should get involved on a more formal basis with extending the availability of the police. This could be on the basis of the social contribution mentioned earlier in the book. The NML (non-market labour) sector could also be involved, for example in patrolling and with watchmen. Just as some countries have a period of military training each year so also might there be police training. Community patrolling and on-call task forces could be organised under the leadership of the police without degenerating into vigilante groups. Many people would welcome the sense of purpose, the comradeship and even the excitement. A careful study of police work would show which duties and activities could be delegated in this way. The concept of enrolled deputies is an old one. It can be badly abused but it could also be developed soundly.

Investigation departments for complaints and the prevention of police corruption would need to be visible and effective. Private security groups should have a cooperative working relationship with the police. The control of riots and protest meetings could be the concern of special squads, as it is in some countries. This would allow more training and would prevent the public-versus-police confrontations that can do so much to damage goodwill and to reduce respect for the law.

In the end one of the most effective aids to police work must be the informer. This is an unattractive concept which conjures up pictures of sneaks at school and Nazi families informing on neighbours they suspected of being Jews. Yet internal information, infiltration and knowing what is going on are much more effective than the post-hoc detective work glamourised in TV serials. I see no problem in drawing a line between intrusion and legitimate 'police intelligence'.

The law

There is need for much pragmatic improvement in the law. There might be a permanent commission that worked to improve the good sense and practicality of the law. This commission would not be run by lawyers – on the contrary it would contain no lawyers. At the first level the commission would consist of members of the public and members of bodies concerned with specific aspects, as they arose, of criminality. Lawyers would only be brought in at a later stage for comment and to put in appropriate form what had already been decided.

There are obvious absurdities in the law which get a lot of public attention and damage the concept of justice. Some of these cause more extensive problems in society. For example in the USA the tradition whereby a lawyer who sues on behalf of a client gets 30 per cent of the damages as a contingency fee has a serious effect on the costs of medical care because of all the unnecessary protective medicine that has to be done. It also clogs the courts with litigation. A simple device would be to suggest that if the claimed damages are reduced by the jury then the lawyer loses his slice first. For example if a million dollar settlement were reduced to half a million then the lawyer would lose the $330,000 he would have got as a contingency fee. This would kill greed and force lawyers to be more realistic. The divorce laws which allow a woman to earn herself up to millions of dollars simply through being married to a rich man for a few years are a glaring absurdity.

We might want to alter our concept of absolute guilt. We might introduce a concept of 'likely guilt'. This is no different in essence from a split jury but it does mean that a jury can, unanimously, bring in a verdict of 'likely guilt'. The penalty would be relatively light or the sentence could even be suspended.

The adversary system could be changed for a more exploratory one in which examiners tried to elicit the facts of the situation in a constructive way. In family law or civil law solutions might be constructed rather than argued through. There is a serious need to do something about the problem of time. Holding things up or stretching them out can constitute a penalty for one of the parties. Time is not neutral. If necessary time must be bought: if one party wants to hold up proceedings then a cost per day will be computed and added to the plaintiff's costs if he loses the case.

The courts

It may be that we shall come to create quite separate courts for dealing with the different types of criminality considered earlier. Just as we have specialists in the medical profession so we would have specialist courts with procedures appropriate to the speciality. This might cut down the huge queues of cases that pile up before courts in some countries today. One slow case would not hold up the queue. Legal procedures may need to be much simplified both to cut the cost and to cut the delays. Lawyers must be among the few professionals who can generate their own work by stretching a case out. Appeals and counter-appeals seem designed more to satisfy lawyers than justice.

The position of lie detection is an interesting one. Suppose the technology is satisfactory and we can show that a person is indeed telling a lie and not just reacting to the stress of his situation in court. Would we be more worried, if there were a false positive, that innocent people would be convicted or that guilty people would escape? The latter would not be such a big worry because we already know that many guilty people are not caught anyway and others are caught and released for want of evidence or on technicalities. A false positive could be checked by repeated testing and if the accused still maintained his innocence then the normal court procedure would take place as it does now.

The one person who knows whether he is guilty or not is the accused. Torture and lie detection are traditional ways of trying to get at that knowledge. Plea bargaining is another – whereby the accused pleads guilty to a lesser crime in order to avoid being charged with a greater one. The process is not much liked by lawyers who are done out of their work. But for certain types of crime the principle would seem to make sense. If the accused pleads guilty there is one type of penalty and if he waits to be proved guilty there is a rather more severe penalty. At first sight the system seems rather unfair on the innocent who would have no option but to proceed to the full trial and the full penalty if found guilty. On the other hand if the principle became well established then the decision to proceed to the next step would be a presumption of innocence. In practice a good deal of this is done, for example with motoring offences and the principle of 'noli contendere' in the USA. On the other hand it seems silly to operate a court as a taxation department. In New York prostitutes are regularly hauled into court, plead guilty, pay a fine and are released. In practical terms it becomes the same as paying a licence fee.

The cost of the legal apparatus can be considerable. In England the cost of the trial of a gang that had stolen £300,000 amounted to far more than that amount. Simplifying procedures, by-passes, new channels and new concepts would be worth considering.

Summary

Law and order are a basic part of the fabric of society. Society needs to give a high priority to this aspect of the quality of life because poor quality here downgrades *everything* else. We tend to regard crime or wrong-doing as 'sin' and to react accordingly. If we can get away from this approach, and regard crime as social pollution then our attitudes and methods can change. For a start we might consider separate types of criminality and deal with each type in a distinct way rather than on a spectrum of severity of sin. One of the prime considerations is not the 'sinfulness' of the crime but the way it affects the quality of life for everyone. The concept of revenge and punishment is replaced by social debt and social pollution. A criminal may have to *earn* his way back to society or be put in an environment that encourages a sense of social responsibility. The concept of giving a pension to ex-prisoners is contrary to moral principles but not to the principle of social pollution.

The status and importance of the police may need increasing. At the same time the general public should be more involved with the police in taking over some functions on a community basis. The law may need modernising by a commission that does not, at first, include lawyers. The police would provide an input to this commission. To use a marketing phrase, there may be 'market segmentation' of the courts with specialised courts dealing with different types of crime. The role of lie detection and guilty pleas may need formalising and developing.

In general, crime should not be acceptable as a necessary tax on living. Tolerance and pragmatism are not contrary to the rule of law. And the effective prevention of crime does not invite a police state. Legislation and the courts are not a game unto themselves but a sanitation service for society.

17 EDUCATION

We come now to the most important area of all. Whatever new concepts and structures we may devise, in the end the quality of society will depend on the quality of its members. That quality is going to be very much influenced by education in the formal sense of the school years and the informal sense of lifelong learning from experience. In most developed countries every person spends his or her most formative years passing through the school system, thus providing a splendid opportunity to develop those skills, perceptions and attitudes that will ensure a positive future.

Yet, if we are brutally frank, our education succeeds at only one task: that of giving children something to do, keeping them occupied and keeping them out of the way. It also provides employment for 476,000 teachers (UK), and provides the largest single item of government expenditure after social security benefits.

There are no villains. The teachers and educators I have met are motivated and energetic – more so than in many other professions. But everyone is locked into a self-sustaining system which generates its own purpose and its own momentum. There is the apostolic succession, in which teachers train and appoint teachers like themselves and in the same subjects. There is the lock-in of continuity, for it is difficult to try something new until it has been tried extensively and it is difficult to try it extensively if it cannot be tried. There is the lock-in of materials, for established publishers are not going to publish materials unless there is a demand and there is no demand if the subject area is not yet established. There is the lock-in of the examinations system, since examinations provide the focus for school work and school work is directed towards these examinations. As mentioned earlier, it is not possible to take an examination in a subject unless there is an examining board, and there is unlikely to be an examining board unless enough schools are taking the exam in the first place. To repeat, there are no villains. Everyone is operating sensibly within his own logic-bubble, which is itself determined by the nature of the system.

Throughout this book I have mentioned, from time to time, systems that have become ends-unto-themselves. To a large extent this has become the case with philosophy, with art, with literature. A game is played with the rules of the game and for the sake of continuing that game – whether or not it contributes much to the world outside the players.

Is the whole purpose of the school system to provide an academic selection system for the few (7.5 per cent of men and 4.5 per cent of women in the UK) who are going on to university? We treat it as such, for everyone at the base of the pyramid is taught with the intention of giving him or her the chance to do well in the exams at the peak of the pyramid.

The problem is a basic one. In itself everything works well. A case can be made for everything that is done. In any case education, like democracy, even if it is faulty is better than anything else. Moreover how can you prove that a new structure would be better? It is impossible to prove that teaching a particular subject is a waste of time because it might just be useful. Many subjects are indeed excellent and the only fault is that far too much time is spent on them. In the end the success of the system can be demonstrated by pointing to the brilliant and able people who have been produced by it. This is the ultimate fallacy: the fallacy of the archway effect. If a stream of brilliant people are seen making their way towards an archway then (surprise, surprise) a stream of brilliant people will be found emerging from that archway even if it has done nothing more than straddle their passage.

A lot of attention has been paid to the administrative structure and politics of education but far less attention has been paid to the content, because people are afraid to express opinions that can be criticised.

The content of education

Almost all of what a child learns at school after the age of ten is totally irrelevant to his needs in later life. What is taught in schools is taught for two very good reasons: it is there, and it has been taught before. The pressure of sheer continuity is enormous. There are Geography teachers to teach Geography and there is a well formulated subject to teach. There are examinations in Geography. Surely Geography is important to give a child a perspective on the world he lives in? The same applies to History and any other subject. Millions of children know about the wives of Henry VIII but hardly any of them know how the corner shop works.

Information is easy to teach so we teach information and we test it in examinations. Process skills, like thinking, are much more difficult to teach and to test, so we tend to ignore them.

Mathematics is an excellent subject and most of our technological development has arisen directly from our development and use of mathematics. I would regard it as the highest expression of human thinking and human achievement. Yet the teaching of mathematics in schools is very largely a waste of time, no matter how excellently it is taught. Some children will require a sound mathematical basis because they are going into subject areas that require this: like engineering or physics.

But they could learn the mathematics required for that as part of their vocational training. Most people use amazingly little mathematics in their ordinary life. If I had to design a subject called mathematics for ordinary life it would include: simple addition and subtraction; the use of decimal notation, multiplication and simple division, the use of a pocket calculator, the handling of elementary percentages, the mathematics of measurement at a basic level. That would be enough. I would leave out all of geometry, trigonometry, algebra, calculus, sets, quadratics and everything else. The amount of time devoted to the teaching of mathematics would be reduced to about one tenth of what it is now. I should, however, teach a lot more about the use of computers. I should develop and teach a subject called 'basic organisation and system behaviour' which would show the mechanics of both.

I would not teach Geography, History or Literature in the formal sense. These would be regarded as background subjects and could be supplemented by Art, Architecture and Anthropology. They would be available on well produced video discs with the internal quality of interest that the television wildlife programmes produced by Anglia Television have. They would be subjects that the children would enjoy exploring just as the very young are fascinated by dinosaurs. Shakespeare would be acted and also observed on top quality video-disc productions but not studied as a set book.

So what would the basic subjects be? The fundamental five would be Reading, Writing, Practical Mathematics, Thinking and Social Skill. Social Skill would not be taught in an academic sense but would be part of school life: getting on with oneself and with others, discipline and achievement. These are the basic skills that a child needs. The skills have to be developed and practised and practised again until there is a high degree of fluency. If education provided nothing more than skill in these basic areas it would have done enough.

The next layer of subject would include the nature of society today. This would not be a matter of intense semi-political discussions on slums or Eskimos but an understanding of the 'nuts and bolts' of ordinary society. It would include broad economics, how business works, how industry works, how government works, how the law works, how cities work, etc. Concepts such as added value, profit, capital, labour and skill would be considered. Simulation games might be used to give the children a feel for interactive process and strategy development. Another subject area would cover the practical development of operating skills: organising, leading, research, getting something done, reporting and like activities. This would be covered in a practical way. Attention would be paid to 'how to get along in society' skills such as getting a mortgage, buying a house, use of libraries, form-filling, protest, use of a solicitor, perhaps motor mechanics. At this stage drama and role playing could be used to increase the understanding of the social skills mentioned amongst the basic subjects. Thinking would be continued as a subject.

All this may seem rather utilitarian but that is a value, not a sneer-word. Many of these subjects would be much more difficult to teach than straightforward knowledge subjects. Attention would need to be given to the structure of the material and the teaching style. As far as possible it should not have to depend on the enthusiasm of a dedicated teacher. It is likely that once a teacher had absorbed the idiom of the subject and acquired some confidence the new subject might prove easier than an old one. I have certainly found this to be the case with teachers who have persevered with the teaching of thinking as a school subject.

There are other subject areas which seem more vague but are also important. For example the use of leisure and what might be called 'happiness' skills. It is not a matter of imparting mechanical skills in the mode of 'we have ways of making you laugh' but more a question of giving consideration to an area in order to replace drift with insight.

Language teaching could be done with total immersion weekends or holiday camp visits to the country or language camps set up as such. Classroom hours seem an ineffective method of teaching.

At university level a vocational subject or a 'culture' subject may have to start at a more basic level since a school start cannot be presumed – but now there would be a stronger motivation to whip through the preliminaries instead of grinding through them at school. This should be much easier if basic learning and thinking skills have been established earlier.

What is the practical likelihood of such a change in the curriculum taking place? In terms of the locked-in system the chances are not high because although an individual teacher or head might want to take some steps in this direction he would soon come up against parents who expected the school to prepare the boy for the currently accepted examinations. One way of making a start might be for industry to decide what sort of people it wanted. At the moment school examinations are solely determined by university requirements but industry as the major employer has a right to make its wishes known. I would suggest an 'industry acceptance examination' which would require demonstrated skill in reading, writing, basic mathematics, thinking and an understanding of how society works. Schools would be obliged to let their pupils take this exam since those who had passed it would be given preference in industrial recruitment. On the whole industry is excessively timid in indicating its needs. The result is that at school there is no understanding at all of how the productive wealth of a country is produced or indeed of the fascination of the business process. In discussing careers, schoolchildren mention a variety of careers from doctor to athlete and from nurse to car mechanic, but industry is hardly mentioned at all. I do not think there is a specific anti-business bias although some teachers are possibly motivated by left-wing ideals. In general the case goes by default since a teacher, herself, has no experience of the industrial process and probably still accepts the idiom of the 'dark satanic mills' that pollute the countryside. Tokenism by industry – in terms of the occasional film strip or special course – is not enough.

In the course of developing Thinking as a school subject we (at the Cognitive Research Trust) noticed that pupils who had not previously been considered bright on an academic basis suddenly turned out to be good thinkers – to the surprise of their teachers and even their peers. It seems that there are pupils who are weak on the 'input' side, that is in taking in concepts and retaining information. Since we usually test the output by reference to the input such pupils would show up badly. In the Thinking lessons, however, the emphasis is not on information but on the use of personal experience. As a result the pupils who were weak on the input side but good at thinking suddenly shone. From this observation arose the examination in General Thinking Skills which we set up to give an opportunity to children to show their skills at thinking independently of a content area. The schools seemed to welcome the idea but after a few sessions it was shelved because of administrative problems regarding the schools' ability to pay the examination expenses.

For some years I have been involved in what seems to be the largest programme in the world for the development of Thinking as a school subject (described in the book, *Teaching Thinking*). About 4,000 schools have acquired the programme or part of it. Some of them have no doubt placed it on the library shelf but others are using it across a wide range of pupil ages and abilities. I am sure the programme could be improved and I am sure that we may develop, in time, better ways of teaching thinking. But what is important is that a start should be made in a practical sense. There should be something for a teacher to use when faced with a class of thirty children on a Monday morning. The programme was funded by a £25,000 grant from the Leverhulme Foundation and a £6,000 grant from the Wates Foundation. There is no funding from the Department of Education or its research arm, the Schools Council, because at first the project was regarded as too speculative and then as too successful to need funds. It seems odd that £356,000 can be spent on developing the pilot's seat for the Concorde and yet this rather important area of education – which some would regard as the very purpose of education – is neglected.

It might just be possible to set up 'New Programme' schools which would use the different curriculum right from the beginning. The interface with examining bodies and universities would be the problem with such an approach.

Television and education

The average youngster in the UK spends nineteen hours a week watching television. By the time he is twenty he may have spent more hours watching television than in school. Some of the television is education either in specific areas (like anthropology) or in the general ways of the world. The Viewdata system now being tried out in the UK by the Post Office would allow a viewer to call up on the television screen one out of millions of pages of possible information, by dialling a number on a hand-held coder. The cost would be about half a penny a page. But of course the motivation has to be there. With video-recorders becoming more readily available in the home there is much scope for home education but again the motivation must be there. The Open University concept in the UK has worked well even though the majority of its students are teachers who may hope to get higher pay if they acquire a degree. When the motivation is there, the technology can cope without any trouble.

In the future the concept of home education may develop. A group of parents may bring their children together for a period each week to make use of television education or video-disc education. Such groups might also go through some of the skills programmes that were not yet widely in use in schools. For example once a week a group of children and parents might meet for an hour to go through the Thinking lessons, one at a time. Such parallel education would fit easily into the concept of the organisation node discussed in the book. Eventually the 'nodes' might set up their own schools.

Teachers and teaching

It may be that in the future teachers will not need to be experts in their own fields. They will be 'people-people' and caretakers of a learning environment. They might in effect become 'private tutors' to a group of children.

So the single teacher would look after the same group of children for all subjects just as is done in the primary school. He would be chosen and trained for his teaching qualifications not for his subject qualifications. This approach would be much easier with the 'New Programme' curriculum than with the present specialised, subject-based curriculum. There is no reason to suppose that a person becomes a good teacher just because he or she becomes expert in a subject area. Anyone who has been at a university knows this very well.

Gifted children

We may need to look for gifted children along many more dimensions than just the academic one. We may want to pay special attention to exceptional personalities – for example leadership qualities or social qualities. With this broader concept of 'giftedness' we should try to make the most productive use of the talents available to society. Does the concept of equality demand that a big man be fed no more than a small man or that both be *equally satisfied* with their food? So special attention to the gifted is not contrary to egalitarianism. This could take the form of special schools for the very gifted. On the other hand it needs to be noted that many children are gifted in only one direction and that excessive emotional dependence on their 'cleverness' may leave them emotional cripples in other matters. The purpose of education must be to produce effective people capable of using their talents, not to produce circus freaks.

Leaving school

A suggestion was made earlier in the book that on leaving school a youngster might be required to spend some time in a sort of national service that could be spent in the NML (non-market-labour) sector. This would develop the discipline of the work habit, the discipline of getting on with others, and the discipline of making a positive contribution to society.

Before career choices had to be made – and they would be made in this period – an extended apprenticeship scheme would be tried. School-leavers would spend several months attached as apprentices in different fields. They would be there not specifically to *learn* that trade but to see what was going on. They would be paid from NML funds but would be expected to make themselves useful to the person who was looking after them. Exposure to a career is much better than reading about it in a career book. Someone who was interested in doing this might be allowed to leave school earlier.

At present momentous career decisions are taken at school. The choice of subjects may have to be determined early, certain exams have to be passed. If a mistake is made then whole careers are excluded for ever. I think we should try to remove this finality of early choices. There should be proper provision for people to come back into the system at a later date and for reasons other than the initial qualifying exam. For example I have suggested earlier in this book that a determined and hard-working person might work his way into university, by-passing the entrance qualifications. Once there, he would be subject to the usual standards demanded but he will have had his opportunity of attempting these standards.

Summary

I have not attempted in this chapter to give a comprehensive blue-print for education. There are many gaps and further thought would refine the suggestions. What I have intended is to suggest that we should not be complacent about education because it satisfies its own criteria of success. I hope I have shown that there are no villains and that it is the locked-in nature of the system that makes it largely a game played unto itself. In terms of its contribution to society, I feel that education – through no fault of the educators – is doing an appalling job and wasting the best opportunity we have for a positive future. I fully acknowledge that change is immensely difficult and that many new notions will be much worse than existing systems and may even lead to chaos. I fully acknowledge that suggestions which depend on all teachers being gifted and highly motivated are unlikely to succeed. I fully acknowledge the dangers of the 'take-off' effect mentioned earlier in the book (a new idea might actually be dangerous until it has acquired enough momentum to lift off). The real question is whether we are prepared vigorously to defend the status quo on the basis that it is the best possible or to acknowledge the need for change while being willing to devote to this crucial area the attention it needs. Just as lawyers are to be excluded from the commission for the improvement of law in its first session, so too we might exclude teachers and educators on the basis that they might simply be inclined to defend their positions rather than explore new ones.

We may need in this endeavour to explore mechanisms of change as much as the content of the change. For example by-pass tracks, 'New Programme' schools, the 'Industrial Acceptance' examination, home education groups and so on. In this area more than in any other the transition problems are enormous and the edge effect is crucial. The finest theory is useless if the very first step can never be taken. I do not believe in wild, if fashionable, experiment but I do not think we will get very far by drift and muddle-through. All the successful innovations in education (such as the polytechnics and the Open University) have happened as a result of definite steps rather than a pious hope that existing institutions would alter.

SUMMARY

In this summary I shall try to crystallise the theme of the book. I shall do this by separating out the basic points so that each can get the attention it needs. There is, however, a considerable degree of overlap. We might start by looking at the three basic points.

1. The quality of life in the future will depend on the quality of our thinking.

To me this seems inescapable. Circumstances and natural events will modify the hopes of our thinking and at times over-ride them completely – but in the end we have nothing else to depend upon. If we do not do our thinking, then drift will do it for us. The question then arises: are we happy with the state of our thinking? I have suggested that we ought not to be, for our habits and style of thinking are largely derived from the disputations of medieval monks. Within the framework of the accepted idiom, there is a great deal of skill and brilliance. But in order to have a positive future we may need to develop a more positive idiom. I am not suggesting that there is an attractive alternative ready for adoption. But I am suggesting that we need to take a cool and objective look at the dangers of the thinking style we never dare challenge.

2. What happens to an organism that evolves characteristics that make further evolution impossible?

Society is an organism that evolves in order to cope with a changing world – even if many of these changes are brought about by its own efforts. If you set a house on fire you have to react to the flames even though you are responsible for them. Nor is it possible to suppose that if we do nothing at all the world will achieve a level of stability.

Many of our institutions have evolved to the point where they may – through no fault of their own – impede further evolution. The same applies to concepts which are but institutions of the mind.

3. Provided our hearts are in the right place, will intelligence, good-will and problem-solving skills be enough?

We have – or could pretend we have – an abundance of these attributes so why should we not tackle the future as it arrives, problem by problem? The many reasons why this traditional approach may not work are listed as separate points elsewhere in this summary. In general, problem-solving, like fault-correcting, cannot provide a new design but just a patched-up old one.

The three basic points have been given above. We can now look at the various problems that can hinder our evolution towards a positive future.

4. There are no villains and no stupid people: there are highly intelligent people acting sensibly within their own logic-bubbles.

I am aware that this is an exaggeration but I have tried, throughout the book, to regard as an axiom the claim that there are no villains or stupid people. It is only too easy to blame problems on villainy or lack of intelligence. That then becomes an exercise in blame and exhortation. Instead, I believe we can explain many of the problems in terms of intelligent people acting intelligently according to the logic of the circumstances in which they find themselves. Collectively the result may be a disaster but an individual improvement in intelligence will not make things better so blame is pointless. To simplify this problem I have introduced the notation of the 'logic-bubble' which covers the total set of perceptions that dictate the logic of the moment. In large part the 'bubble' will be created by the rules of the structure within which the actor is placed. Most often people are locked in by structures and act sensibly within them. That is why we get such paradoxes as Catch-22, Catch-23 and Catch-24. It is clear (Catch-23) that something may need doing but that it never makes sense to do it at any particular moment.

5. It is not the destination that matters but the very next step
    that has to be taken.

Much of our utopian thinking is concerned with ultimate destinations. Yet there is no hope of reaching these destinations if the next step is impossible or unacceptable. To provide this obvious concept with the attention it merits I have coined the term 'the edge effect'. It is at the edge of action that we must focus our thinking, not on an ideal assembly of abstract notions that make up the architecture of a dream.

6. Can we afford to rely upon evolution through drift and crisis
    management or through the use of general 'compass' directions?

We can throw up our hands at the complexity of the future and just manage each crisis and hope to muddle through in the end – like a bridge player who survives his bad hands and hopes for better cards to be dealt. We may feel that complexity denies us any alternative since a planned future would be even more dangerous. In practice we tend to do a little better than mere drift. We establish certain guiding principles as 'compass' directions and at every decision point we choose the right compass direction. This is sensible strategy but I have tried to show at the beginning of the book why it can be dangerous. There may be times when we might have to turn 'South' in order to be able to continue our journey 'North'. Are we prepared to turn away from some general principles, in order eventually to enjoy them more fully? In a democratic system with a short time-scale is it possible to take an action which has an initial negative phase? Or does political expediency make this forever impossible?

7. Powerful battle-cries are not necessarily effective operating principles.

Battle-cries sometimes provide the 'compass' directions mentioned above. A battle-cry or a slogan may be useful to highlight a grievance or to give a direction, but as an operating principle it may not be effective. A compass will indicate the North but a bicycle is more useful for getting there. We are good at guiding principles for protest but far less good at guiding principles for action. Very often in the evolution of society we are forced to use battle-cries as slogans and then we get confused when we try to use them as operating principles. We need to be rather more clear about the distinction.

8. Whichever way we look at it there remains an appallingly negative bias to our thinking style.

There are a lot of practical and historical reasons for this and I have considered them in detail in the book. The more one looks into it the more extraordinary does the phenomenon appear. I believe it to be derived directly from the thinking style used in medieval theological disputes to crush heresies on an intellectual level. That style came to dominate our educational establishments and so dictated the idiom we still use. We often tend to forget its peculiar nature and to suppose it to be the only thinking style possible. We acclaim the critical intelligence and propose it as the ultimate aim of education. We operate the adversary system whenever we can and admire debating skills and dialectical argument. There are many practical reasons for this negative bias: to be destructive is easier and more immediately satisfying than to be constructive; destruction is itself immune from further attack. Protest can be highly effective and society needs the conscience role that protest offers. Yet somehow we have to accept that constructive and creative ideas need to emerge from somewhere. It is no use pruning if we are unable to plant. The real tragedy is that many brilliant minds trained to this idiom of negativity might have been just as brilliant – and far more useful to society – if they had been encouraged in a more positive idiom. We falsely believe that negative-design is enough: that is to say the improvement of a design by correcting the faults and dealing with the inadequacies. But we also need positive-design and that includes changing the basic concept, not just trimming the existing one.

9. The problem of complacency: how can you be convinced the present idea is not good enough if you cannot conceive of there being any alternative?

Man has a right to be smug and satisfied with his progress. Yet compared to the potential that technology has provided I feel that our progress is not much to be happy about. Complacency is a problem that arises directly from our negative style of thinking. You must prove that something is wrong before you earn the right to think of an alternative. But quite often something is good – but not good enough. With the negative style that is the end of thinking, for a successfully defended concept is thought to exclude any better alternative. With a more positive style of thinking we might be able to acknowledge the excellence of what is – and still set out to think about improvement or change If we do not set out to think up a new concept in the first place how can we find the concept that will show that it was worth setting out to find an alternative?

10. Many an institution in any evolved society has become an end unto itself and no longer contributes to society.

It is not enough that an institution should satisfy its own criteria of excellence. Philosophy, art, literature, education and the universities have all evolved their own framework of justification and they seek to play the rules as they have written them and to congratulate themselves on a success they have defined for themselves. Whether this definition of success has any relevance to society at large is another matter. When something becomes an end unto itself it can become a parasite on society for it absorbs money and the most brilliant minds but provides nothing in return. The players enjoy the game for its own sake. Like a spinning star the body whirls forever around its own axis. Rather too much of the productive talent of society is locked up in such bodies that have become ends unto themselves. Witness the lack of impact that the many university departments of philosophy have on ordinary life. It is high time that art, literature and philosophy came back into the main stream of life.

11. What is urgent will always take precedence over what is important.

There are always so many urgent things to do and so many urgent problems to be solved that there is never any time to consider matters that may be important. This is a particular instance of Catch-23. The problem also arises from our emphasis on 'reactive-thinking' rather than 'projective-thinking'. We train ourselves to react to problems, to collect information and then to react to this. We are more comfortable reacting than projecting our minds forwards to create and construct. We are problem solvers rather than opportunity seekers. This tendency is especially dangerous since so many of our institutions, such as management training schools, see their role as the development of problem-solving skills.

It may seem strange that part of the book should be concerned with 'attacking' our negative habits of mind for that very 'attack' must itself seem an exercise of what is being attacked. Yet my intention is not to attack but to illuminate. I think we should become aware of those habits of mind that we take for granted. I think we should become aware of the restrictions we place upon ourselves. I think we should be made aware of complacency. All these things have a value and a place in society and it would be absurd to 'attack' them. Critical assessment is invaluable in order to prevent us making fools of ourselves. My point is that these habits have come to dominate our thinking to the exclusion of everything else and that is a danger – and dangers need pointing out. In continuing the summary we can look at some of the more positive points.

12. An organisation revolution is going to succeed the industrial revolution.

We cannot cope with complexity by hoping that it will go away of its own accord. The world is inevitably going to get more complex as we become able to do more, need more and want more. For example the suggestion of alternative life-styles and alternative work patterns will greatly increase complexity. The only answer to complexity is organisation. The computer has come only just in time to provide us with the perfect means of dealing with complexity. So the organisational revolution can get under way. The trouble is that most people are terrified of the idea of organisation because we perceive a direct clash between organisation and freedom. This is a nonsense that must be tackled directly. There are different sorts of organisation: some are indeed restricting but others are freedom enhancing (for example the airline computer system that allows you to switch routes in a matter of seconds). Anarchy is only freedom for predators. We must take immense care that organisation should be used to simplify life and make people more free rather than the other way round. We must take immense care that the computer is not used just to make possible complicated schemes that restrict freedom. We must take care to see that the potential of the computer is used to simplify life. We must get this concept of organisation very clear because our future is going to depend upon it.

13. The concept of 'nodes' and 'nodalism'.

The tone of this book has been against 'big government' but in favour of organisation. I have therefore put forward the concept of 'nodalism' in order to provide a concrete suggestion as to how it is possible to be against central government but for organisation. I have not gone into detail as to how the concept might work and it could be worked up in much greater detail. Nodalism is a sort of 'functional tribalism'. People are connected together not by geography but by their desire to have organised for them the basic framework of life so that they can be more free. The organising node is a slave – not a master. A node would be a sort of computer 'village', for the computer would provide the organising framework. Around the node develops a community that can share and organise; assess its own priorities and make its own decisions. Alternative life styles and work patterns would fit naturally into the framework. Eventually the nodes would become alternative mini-governments and a person might switch his allegiance from one to another depending on his needs and life style. He would 'vote' with his feet. The implications of the concept are extensive. The technology is to hand.

14. There are many areas in which we need to develop new concepts.

In this book I have not wished to offer 'gee-whiz' concepts for the future. I am aware of the Catch-22 effect of creativity: 'If the concepts are way-out they will be acclaimed as creative but condemned as impractical: if the concepts are practical then they will be condemned as ordinary and non-creative.' I do not think there are any concepts – however wonderful – which we could accept as blue-prints for the future, because we would have no way of assessing their worth. I have, however, put forward a number of concepts: the 'trinity' concept for industrial organisation; the concept of 'profit per head'; the concept of 'unowned capital'; the non-market-labour (NML) concept; the concept of the 'timid currency'; the 'tandem economy'; the segmentation of crime as 'social pollution' rather than sin; and the 'New Programme' curriculum for schools – among others. The purpose of these suggestions is to show that it is possible to change some of our accepted concepts. Some of the concepts may have merit if developed further. Others may serve only as a provocation.

15. We ought formally to acknowledge the role of provocation in thinking.

This is difficult within the framework of our traditional thinking idiom. In many of my other books I have dealt at length with the role of provocation in creativity. There is no mystique about it. In a patterning system provocation is perfectly logical. In this book I have repeated the 'po' concept and I have also suggested – for the first time – a punctuation device that could facilitate the entry of provocation into written language. Most people are aware of the value of provocation in the development of new ideas – for how else are we to step outside the established frameworks? – but we are hesitant about formal recognition of this necessary part of constructive thinking. If we are going to give more emphasis to this aspect of thinking we are going to need to develop the basic concepts. For example instead of immediately rejecting an offered idea I would like to see a listener capable of treating it as a provocation that might lead to a further idea. Creativity is not a mystical gift but the willingness to explore provocations forward until they begin to make sense. Provocation is as basic as analysis.

16. In general we need to pay a lot more attention to the development of thinking skills.

For too long have we tended to regard thinking as 'intelligence in operation'. Yet intelligence alone does not ensure effective thinking skills and in some cases (the 'intelligence trap') it may even be counter-productive. We tend to emphasise cleverness rather than wisdom. We tend to emphasise logical processing rather than perceptual breadth. We tend to emphasise reactive thinking rather than projective thinking. At several points I have mentioned the on-going programme that has been developed for use in the school curriculum to counter these tendencies and to give some direct attention to thinking. At the very least I believe that we ought to pay as much attention to practical thinking skills as to philosophy. We should regard thinking as a skill that can be developed and a tool that can be applied in a deliberate manner.

17. We need to be specific about providing mechanisms for change.

It is unreasonable to expect an executive to risk damaging his established operations by diverting part of his budget to trying something new. He needs a discretionary budget with which to experiment. It is unreasonable to expect those within an institution to encourage activities which run counter to the establishment of that institution. There is a need for by-passes. It is unreasonable to expect a manager to be an entrepreneur. We need to foster entrepreneurial effort, not just leave it to fight its way through. We need to nurse new ideas and let them develop to the stage where their potential can be assessed. We need to develop test-beds for ideas, for otherwise an idea can only be judged within the existing framework of experience and its potential will be missed if it is the sort of idea that changes frameworks. We need to encourage plurality, options and choices rather than seek to standardise development. Above all we need to dispel the myth that there is enough creative constructive effort around and that a good idea will have its due effect.

18. We need to develop new concepts: some brand new and some just slightly different.

The killer phrase in creativity is 'the same as...' for the novelty in a new idea can be forgotten as the similarity with an old idea is commented upon. Do we concentrate on the 80 per cent that is similar or the 20 per cent that is different? Sometimes it is necessary to shift a concept slightly in order to allow our minds to develop new lines of thought. For example the concept of 'earned freedom' is only slightly different from that of ordinary freedom, but the implications are very different. When we shift a concept we often need to 'freeze' this shift with a new term, otherwise we cannot hold it. Similarly we may need to give a term to a collection of notions that each exist separately. For example there is nothing new in the idea of the three parallel goods: good for me; good for society; good for tomorrow. But the development of a concept like 'bonism' allows the package to be carried around instead of assembled each time. There is always the danger of developing jargon for the sake of jargon but sometimes we need new expressions. In fact we never need a new expression in order to *describe* something for that can usually be done by a combination of old expressions. But in order to use thought as an *operating* system we may need new expressions.

19. In the end mood is more important than anything else.

Does mood arise from circumstance, from habit or from an ideological framework? Which is preferable: ambition and striving or adjustment and contentment? There are no easy answers. We know that purpose, achievement, framework and self-image are important. We know how to make people miserable but are not convinced that people know how to make themselves happy. I have dealt at length with this problem of mood and happiness in a previous book (*The Happiness Purpose*) and so I have not thought it necessary to repeat that material in this book. The danger of the 'chemical' mood that might be induced by TV or by the complexity of society needs careful study. Operating moods such as the 'jungle mood' or the 'nursery mood' are easily changeable depending on such things as media and pop culture.

20. Education has a major role to play in the development of a positive future.

There are no villains in education. Instead there is a locked-in system that has evolved to satisfy its own requirements. The edge effect is so strong that change of any sort is difficult. Moreover, how can it ever be shown that change will be better than the existing state of affairs? So the problems are immense. I do not think there is much hope of changing the whole system at one time. I think there is a need for alternative tracks. I also think there is a great need for attention to such controlling points as university entrance examinations which dominate the school curriculum. In the future I think the academic side of education is going to be much less important than the people-developing side. I would not expect the necessary changes in education to come from within the system – not through lack of talent but because anyone within the system is locked in to the system as it exists.

21. Can we develop a positive attitude towards a positive future?

This whole book is based on the belief that we can. We may need to overcome the restrictions of some of our more enjoyable negative habits. We may need to throw out some traditional concepts and re-stock with some more suitable ones. We may need to pay much more attention to the structures within which people are locked. In addition to a general positive attitude we can develop some specific positive concepts like plurality, simplicity, effectiveness, organisation and even discipline. Instead of fatalism, pessimism and optimism, a positive attitude suggests that man is master of his fate – not because he has found a new ideology but because he is prepared to work positively towards a positive future. There is a lot of talent and energy available.

Conclusion

This book was never meant to be a blue-print for a positive future. We cannot design the future for there is too much uncertainty. But we can design our attitudes so that they are positive and flexible and will allow us to make a fuller use of the benefits which technology has provided. In the end material goods do not matter as much as people-values, but ultimately productive wealth is necessary to give us the time and freedom to escape from the tyranny of mere survival. We need to do a lot of thinking. But before that we have to consider whether we are locked into structures and concepts that prevent positive development. If so, we can no longer wait for drift and crisis management to carry us forward to a better future; instead we have to make a deliberate and positive effort to secure a positive future. The call is to arms: not the outmoded arms of gun and bomb but the focused power of human thinking unleashed from its pettiness.

INDEX

Note: Page references in *italics* indicate illustrations.

239